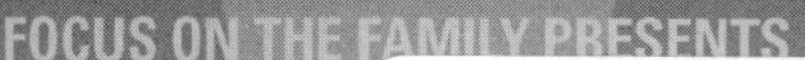
FOCUS ON THE FAMILY PRESENTS

90 Devotions for Kids

MARSHAL YOUNGER & KATHY BUCHANAN

Tyndale House Publishers, Inc.
Carol Stream, Illinois

90 Devotions for Kids, Volume 2

ISBN: 978-1-58997-677-1

A Focus on the Family book published by
Tyndale House Publishers, Inc., Carol Stream, Illinois 60188

Editor: Marianne Hering
Cover design by Jacqueline L. Nuñez
Cover illustration and interior illustrations of characters by Gary Locke
Interior design by Lexie Rhodes

Library of Congress Cataloging-in-Publication information is available for this book by contacting http://catalog.loc.gov/help/title-keyword.htm.

Printed in the United States of America

1 2 3 4 5 6 7 8 9 /18 17 16 15 14

For manufacturing information regarding this product, please call 1-800-323-9400.

Contents

How to Use These Devotions

Welcome to the *90 Devotions for Kids* from the book of Matthew. I'm excited to be going through the life of Jesus with you for the next three months.

This book takes you through the entire book of Matthew. There are only a handful of verses that we skipped, and the devotionals go pretty much in the same order as the biblical text. If you are younger than age nine, I recommend that you go through this devotional with your parents. There are some difficult verses to understand, and your parents will probably do a fantastic job explaining them to you. If you decide to do the lessons without your parents, make sure you write down any questions you might have and ask someone later. I wouldn't want you to go too long with a question on your mind.

It's very important that you read the Scripture passage before you go through each devotional. Every day makes a reference to the Bible reading, and so the devotional by itself may not make sense without it. One of your goals in reading this book is to begin the habit of reading your Bible every day, if you're not already. Studying the Word of God daily is a key to growing in your relationship with Jesus.

Hopefully this book will be helpful in giving you the "big picture" about Jesus' life. Sometimes we know random stories and verses, but it's also beneficial to learn about the entire life of Jesus, in order, from His beautiful birth to His roller-coaster ministry to His agonizing death to His glorious resurrection. (Oops! I gave away the ending!) By the end of these ninety days, I hope you can learn to appreciate our Savior and Lord, Jesus Christ, even more.

—John Avery Whittaker

Devo 1

One Messy Family Tree

Read Matthew 1:1–17.

Wally Haggler wants to do what is right. But sometimes he thinks he can't, because his family is full of convicted criminals. In the Adventures in Odyssey episode "The Green Ring Conspiracy, Part I" (album 53), Wally learns that even though he can't control the actions of his relatives, he can choose to take charge of his life and do good things.

Wally isn't the only one with a family full of unsavory and shady characters. Even Jesus had some shady characters in His family. Today's Scripture passage contains a record of Jesus' ancestors. It's more than a list of funny names that are difficult to pronounce. God put that list in the Bible because He wanted to show us something important about Jesus' ancestors.

All the people on that list played a part in many Old Testament stories. Some of these people were heroes, and some were disappointments. Some were good and honorable. Others were known for lying, cheating, disobeying God, and even committing murder.

It makes you wonder why God would want His perfect Son to come from a family tree with rotten branches. Wouldn't God want Jesus' family to be filled with perfect people who were known for doing wonderful things?

But that's not the way God works. He uses imperfect people to carry out His purposes in the world. He also brings good from bad situations. Jesus came in all His goodness and glory to bring hope to a messy world—starting with a messy manger in a messy stable.

Loquacious Learning with Eugene

One of Jesus' most well-known ancestors was King David. He was known for being a courageous man who loved God. (Remember the story about David and Goliath in the Bible? David used a slingshot and the power of God to kill the disreputable Philistine.) David was even called "a man after [God's] own heart" (1 Samuel 13:14). And yet this same man plotted the murder of a loyal soldier named Uriah so he could marry Uriah's wife! That isn't exactly the kind of behavior you'd expect from a king who said he followed God, is it? But God forgave David when he repented of his sins. David's life is a beautiful example of how God can bring good from our mistakes if we ask His forgiveness.

Jesus' lineage shows us that God can do amazing things, no matter what. He can use far-from-perfect people to make His perfect plans come about.

Daily Challenge

Ask your parents to tell you stories about your grandparents or even your great-grandparents. Talk about what you can learn from the wise choices and mistakes your relatives have made.

Devo 2

A New Name

Read Matthew 1:18–25.

What would you think if you came to school one day, and everyone started calling you the Kid Who Always Has Pizza for Lunch? What if your family called you the Child Who Leaves Her Dirty Socks on the Floor? And your neighborhood friends called you the One Who Always Wants to Go Swimming? What if people named you by the things you do?

You probably would change your behavior so you could be known as the Kid Who Always Gets Good Grades in Math or the One Who Usually Has Kind Words.

Did you know that God has a whole bunch of names in the Bible? Because He is so big and powerful and so many other great things, He can't be fully described by a single name. He's called *El Shaddai*, which means "God Almighty";[1] *Jehovah Jireh*, which means "provider";[2] *Elohim*, which means "strong one";[3] and many other names.

In Matthew 1 we discover a new name for God that was given to His Son, Jesus. Did you see it when you read today's Bible passage? Yep, there it is in verse 23: *Immanuel*. "God with us."[4] The name *Immanuel* describes a God who walks with us and knows us personally. It's not like the names for God in the Old Testament. Those make Him sound a little scary because He's so powerful and so far above us.

Jesus came to earth as Immanuel—*God with us*. He ate and drank with the poor and with people who were outcasts. He laughed heartily as He sat around telling His disciples stories. He shed tears when He saw someone in pain. He felt loneliness and fear and pain. Jesus walked alongside people and felt their feelings. He showed that God loves us and wants a relationship with us.

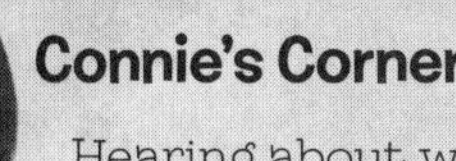

Connie's Corner

Hearing about what all the names of God mean made me wonder what my own name means. So I did some research and found out that my formal name, *Constance*, means "steadfast." I kind of like that meaning, since I'm so consistent. You know, always on time, steady, even-tempered. On second thought, maybe it's not so much a description of who I am right now, but a good reminder of who I want to become.

In the *Odyssey* adventure "Back to Bethlehem, Part 1" (album 10), Connie and Eugene witness the birth of Jesus when they travel to the Holy Land in the Imagination Station. They see for themselves that Jesus is born into a common life, and that His parents are ordinary people. His humble life on earth is a far cry from His royal home in heaven. But coming to earth as a human doesn't change who Jesus has always been. He is still the all-knowing, all-powerful Creator and King of the universe.

The people of Jesus' time couldn't grasp that God chose to come to earth in human form so that He could walk among us. We can now call Jesus the Amazing God Who Came to Earth to Love Ordinary People Like You and Me!

Daily Challenge

In what ways is Jesus Immanuel, "God with us," in your daily life? How is He with you at school? When you're doing chores? When you're at a baseball game? What special name could you give to Jesus that captures how much you appreciate His closeness to you?

Devo 3

What to Get the God Who Has Everything

Read Matthew 2:1–12.

Gold. Frankincense. Myrrh.

These seem like strange gifts for a baby, don't they? Why didn't the wise men bring Jesus a cuddly blanket and a stuffed giraffe instead? But these gifts carried a special meaning and importance, perhaps even more than the wise men themselves realized. Here's why.

Gold was a gift that people in Bible times gave to honor a king.[1] The men from the East recognized Jesus as a child who would one day be a king. The wise men brought Jesus their most precious gifts to honor Him.

Frankincense was a costly, sweet-smelling gum from a tree that people offered as a gift to worship God.[2] Frankincense was burned during Jewish religious services, and the fragrance would fill the temple.

Myrrh was a symbol of bitterness, sorrow, and pain. It was also used to prepare bodies for burial. The wise men couldn't have known how Jesus would die, and yet they brought Him this gift.[3]

Giving the three gifts showed that the wise men honored Jesus as King and worshipped Him as God. These gifts also foreshadowed (gave a hint about the future) that one day Jesus would experience the sorrow and pain of death.

It's harder for us to come up with gift ideas for Jesus. We can't follow a star to heaven or ship Him a package via FedEx. What would we send Him anyway? He owns all the chocolate and music and electronic games in the world already!

But there is one gift we can give Him.

Here's a hint: Hebrews 13:15 says, "Let us continually offer to God a sacrifice

Wandering with Wooton

Sometimes when the weather's crummy and my mailbag is heavy, I start to get grumpy. But I've learned that if I start looking around at things to be thankful for, it's hard to stay in a bad mood.

So I'll say, "God, thanks for the squirrels—even if they drop nuts on my head. And thank You for the rain that waters Mrs. Fenwick's tulips. And thanks for the snow, even if it's really, really cold, because it'll make for great sledding when I'm done with my route. Thanks, too, for warm clothes and for my yummy cinnamon-licorice chili that I'll get to make when I get home!" After thanking God for all these things, pretty soon I'm singing happy songs again.

Of course, then Mrs. Fenwick comes out and tells me I'm singing too loud and it's waking her cat. But that's okay. I'm even thankful for cats!

of praise." And Psalm 95:2 tells us, "Let us come to him and give him thanks. Let us praise him with music and song" (NIRV).

God loves it when we praise Him for everything He's done.

So let's give Him a gift He'll really appreciate. Send up a King-sized "You're awesome, God!" prayer of praise.

Daily Challenge

The book of Psalms is filled with poems and songs of praise and thanks to God. Write your own poem or compose a song about Jesus that reveals why He's important to you.

Devo 4

Power Plays

Read Matthew 2:13–23.

Every once in a while, you'll see a news report on TV about a huge forest fire. A video camera shows a man clutching his garden hose in his backyard, ready to fight the towering blaze with a trickle of water.

That's what the story of Herod is about in today's Bible reading. Herod was a very powerful king, but he was no match for God! After Jesus was born, Herod tried to stop God's plans by killing all the baby boys in Israel, but it didn't work. Like fighting a fire with a garden hose, Herod learned that God was much too powerful for him to take on.

Herod wasn't the only one who tried to outsmart God. Some people in Old Testament times thought they could build a tower to heaven so they would be as powerful as God (see Genesis 11:1–8). Another time, the priests of Baal thought they could prove that their god was more powerful than Elijah's God. So they prayed to Baal and asked him to send down fire from heaven (1 Kings 18:16–38). And Pharaoh thought that he could make the Israelites stay in Egypt as his slaves (Exodus 5:1–8).

But guess what? No one had the power to change God's plans. And neither do we. No matter what we do, God never says, "Wow! I didn't see that coming. Guess I'll try something else." We can ignore God or disobey Him or turn away from Him, but it never works!

God helped Joseph and Mary keep Jesus alive by sending them all to Egypt. God will work out His plans with or without us—but it's a lot more rewarding to be a part of His plans! We can't wreck God's plans any more than King Herod could. It's like trying to put out a forest fire with a garden hose!

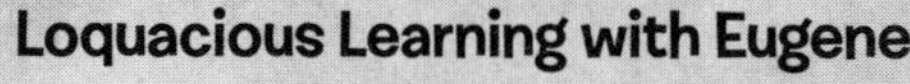

Loquacious Learning with Eugene

Consider these statistics: The sun is believed to be approximately 864,938 miles in diameter,[1] and it's not even one of the largest stars! So far, scientists have discovered more than 370,000 species of beetles.[2] And the human brain contains close to 100 billion nerve cells,[3] which increase in number as you learn new things. If God is powerful enough to create all these things, I'm quite certain He can handle any problems we might have.

In the *Odyssey* episode "The Power of One" (album 44), a Kids' Radio broadcast includes a rhyming tale about Samson to highlight God's power. God gives Samson great power, but Samson starts to think his power is his own, not God's. Samson eventually learns the hard way that God is the One with all the power! (Check out the true story of Samson in Judges 13–16.)

Here's an idea: Learn from other people's mistakes, and don't challenge God!

Daily Challenge

At the top of a sheet of paper, write out Philippians 4:13: "I can do everything through him who gives me strength." Always remember that God can give you the courage and strength you need.

Devo 5

Brave Words

Read Matthew 3:1–12.

Today, the Italian astronomer Galileo is called "the father of modern science." Back in the 1600s, he was known as a great scientist. But did you know that he was also a convicted criminal?

Galileo studied the planets and stars, and he also discovered that the sun, not the earth, was the center of the solar system. At the time, people believed that the sun, stars, and other plants revolved around the earth. But Galileo insisted that the earth moved around the sun! When Galileo tried to persuade people that his special knowledge was true, the religious leaders put him on trial. The court convicted Galileo of spreading lies (heresy), and he spent the last nine years of his life under house arrest.

Can you believe it? Galileo was thrown in prison for being right about the earth! And he was actually the one who was right! His special knowledge was accurate.

John the Baptist was also right. He didn't know much about the solar system, but he knew a lot about Jesus. Like Galileo, John was unpopular with the religious leaders of his day, who were called Sadducees and Pharisees. John was unpopular not just because he wore odd clothes and ate locusts (which is definitely weird!). People also disliked him because God gave him special knowledge about who Jesus was, and John was brave enough to talk about it.

John told everyone who came to the desert, "After me will come one who is more powerful than I, whose sandals I am not fit to carry" (Matthew 3:11). He also told people that Jesus would "[burn] up the chaff with unquenchable fire" (verse 12). That fire language was code for "God's going to judge you unless you

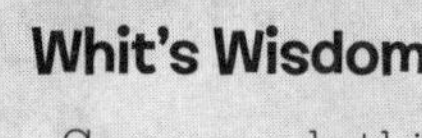

Whit's Wisdom

Some people think that John the Baptist invented baptism, but it was actually practiced many years before John the Baptist or Jesus entered the picture. Baptism symbolizes washing sin away. The people John baptized were showing that they were sorry for their sins and wanted to change (repent). After Jesus died and was raised to life again, baptism took on a new meaning. Christians are baptized to publicly proclaim that we have died with Christ (by going into the water) and have been resurrected with Him (by coming out of the water). It's an outward sign that we have been saved and have made a commitment to follow Christ.

say you're sorry for doing wrong, and stop doing it." Many people listened to John, but many powerful people thought he was wrong. (Sneak preview: In the next chapter of Matthew, John lands in jail!)

Because of Galileo's bravery, scientists in the seventeenth century could study the solar system in a new way. And because John the Baptist (and others after him) was brave enough to tell people about Jesus, we can all know the special knowledge about God.

Daily Challenge

What special knowledge do you have about Jesus? What does the New Testament say about Him? Make a list of what Jesus has done for you and your family. Think of three friends or family members who need to know about Jesus. Then be brave enough to tell them about Him.

Devo 6

Stamp of Approval

Read Matthew 3:13–17.

Imagine that your team is in the state basketball championship. You have only five seconds to win the game for Mid-America Middle School. You take a quick glance at the scoreboard. The ball is in your hands, and your team is trailing 48 to 50. You tune out the shouts from the crowd and the screech of sneakers against the wood court. You even ignore the player in front of you, who is waving his arms to keep you from taking a shot.

There's no way you can pass to anyone. So you shoot the ball from center court toward the hoop. The buzzer sounds. The gymnasium falls silent as the ball rolls around the rim twice and then three times . . . and then drops in! A three-pointer and a big win!

Immediately your teammates lift you onto their shoulders. You search the crowd, looking for the one person you want to see cheering for you. Not the principal or your coach or the cute classmate you have a crush on. There he is! He's wearing a yard-long grin and waving an upturned thumb. Your dad. And Mom is right beside him, jumping up and down and screaming your name.

Most of us want to make our parents proud. And even though we don't always agree with everything they say (like "You're grounded!" or "Clean your room"), it's super-important to us that our parents think well of us.

When Jesus was baptized, His Father in heaven gave His approval by sending down His Spirit in the form of a dove (Matthew 3:16). The dove landed on Jesus as God the Father spoke from heaven for all to hear: "This is my Son, whom I love; with him I am well pleased" (verse 17).

Connie's Corner

Since my parents' divorce years ago, I don't see my dad very often. And it sometimes hurts to know that he's not around to teach me how to fix a flat tire or laugh at my corny jokes or just pat me on the shoulder and tell me he's proud of me. I'm grateful that Whit has been a father figure to me, but I've also learned to lean on God more when I miss having a dad around. I know God loves me more than any human father ever could, and even when I make mistakes (which, I admit, sometimes happens), He still loves me and is proud to call me His daughter.

With those words, God claimed Jesus as His very own Son and showed that He was proud of Jesus. This happened even before Jesus had performed any miracles or preached any sermons! Jesus was baptized to set an example for us. He was already perfect and didn't need to have His sins forgiven. But He was baptized to show the importance of loving and obeying God.

You also make God proud when you make wise choices. His smile is a mile long when He sees you caring for others. He cheers when you choose to act Christlike even though it's hard. He understands that you're going to mess up, and He doesn't expect you to be perfect—that's Jesus' job. But remember, when you do obey His words, you're not only helping yourself live better, but you're also making your heavenly Dad really proud. And His approval is way more important than anyone else's.

Daily Challenge

List some words that describe what fathers should be like. Maybe *caring*, *strong*, and *a good example* are a few of the words on your list. Then jot down some examples of how God is like a father to you.

Devo 7

Fighting Back

Read Matthew 4:1–11.

Imagine innocently stepping outside your house on a snowy day. The air is crisp; the deep banks of snow are sparkling in the sunlight. Then suddenly . . . *SPLAT!* You get smacked in the back of the head with a snowball. Then more snowballs come at you. *Splat! Splat! Splat!* You run around the side of the house and peer around the corner, and from there you see the problem. On the other side of the yard, your brother has made a pile of snowballs as tall as he is. Uh-oh . . . you're in trouble now!

The first thing you need is a way to defend yourself. That's why you're hiding behind the house. But you'll also need to fight back with some snowballs of your own. A lot of them!

Jesus had a similar experience when the devil tempted Him in the wilderness. Jesus was weak from not eating for forty days. Then all of a sudden, the devil threw temptation after temptation at Him. *Splat! Splat! Splat!* Did you notice how Jesus handled these three temptations? He fought back with "ammunition" from God's Word! It's just like having a pile of snowballs ready to throw back at your brother.

In the *Odyssey* episode "The Devil Made Me Do It" (album 32), Satan's lies are exposed during the Slimy Awards, and believers are shown how to fight temptation. During the ceremony, awards are given to the best demons in the industry. But technical difficulties (God's Word) prevent the show from continuing.

You, too, can use the ammunition of God's Word to fight temptation. Memorize Bible verses one at a time—just like making snowballs. For instance, the next

Whit's Wisdom

One of my favorite verses about temptation is 1 Corinthians 10:13, which says, "God is faithful; he will not let you be tempted beyond what you can bear. But when you are tempted, he will also provide a way out so that you can endure."

time you're tempted to call your sister a name because she's being incredibly annoying, just remind yourself, "Anyone who has knowledge controls his words. A man who has understanding is not easily upset" (Proverbs 17:27, NIRV).

God has given you a whole Book of truth to fight the lies of the enemy. So use it—just like Jesus did!

Daily Challenge

Ask a friend to help you memorize Scripture. You can practice reciting verses to each other. Some great verses to start with are John 3:16, Ephesians 2:8–9, Romans 8:28, Psalm 27:1, Proverbs 3:5–6, Philippians 4:6–7, and Matthew 5:16. Ask your parents or a youth leader for more ideas.

Jesus' Family Tree

Fill in this crossword with the names of some famous and not-so-famous ancestors of Jesus. To find the names of some of the people, you'll have to look up a Bible verse first. We've filled in two names for you (Amminadab and Zerah).

Genesis 17:9 ________
Abijah
Ahaz
Amminadab
Amon
Azor
2 Samuel 5:4 ________
Eleazar
Eliakim
2 Chronicles 29:20 ________
Hezron
Isaac
Genesis 25:31 ________
Jeconiah
Jehoram
Jesse
Joseph
Genesis 43:3 ________

Luke 1:30 ________
Obed
Perez
Joshua 6:17 ________
Ram
Ruth 1:16 ________
Salmon
1 Kings 3:8-10 ________
Tamar
Uzziah
Zerah
Haggai 2:4 ________ (This name starts with a Z. Spell it carefully!)

Puzzle #1

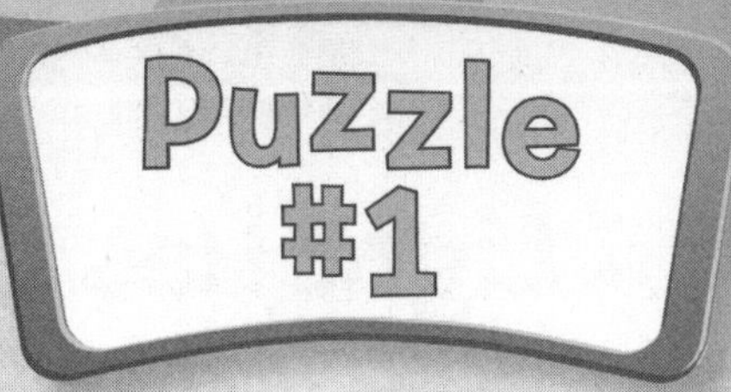

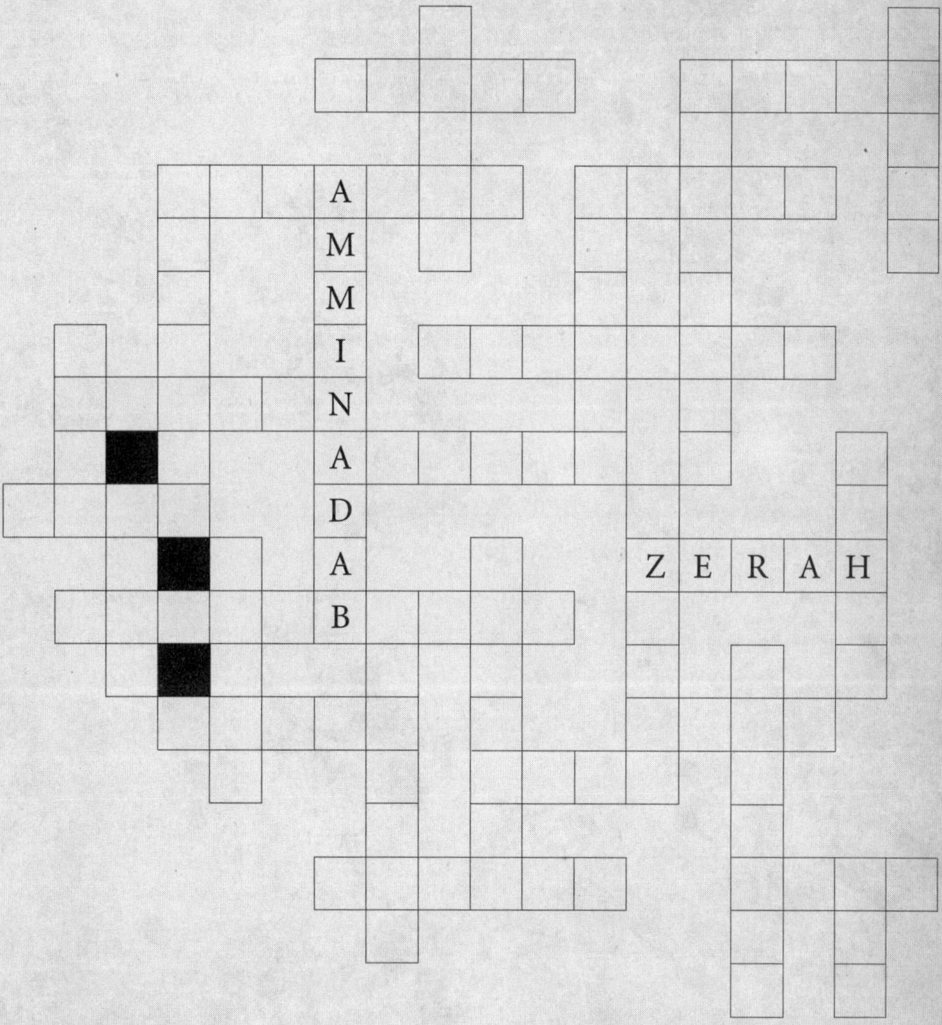
AMMINADAB
ZERAH

Answers on page 208.

Devo 8

A Light Has Dawned

Read Matthew 4:12–17.

Jesus was born in a dark time and place. Life was hard for the Jewish people, and they had a lot of struggles. Many were poor, and growing food could be difficult, especially for those who didn't own land. If a person borrowed money from someone and couldn't pay it back, the lender was allowed to take away the person's children and sell them as slaves. Or the lender could lock up the poor person in prison indefinitely. People who were sick or handicapped were considered unclean. That meant they weren't allowed to go to the temple or synagogues. They were never to be touched. In some cases, it meant that sick people had to leave their families and live outside of town.

The Romans, who ruled over the Jewish people, were cruel. The Roman government charged the Jewish residents very high taxes and also made strict and unfair rules for the people to obey. In today's Bible passage, King Herod threw John the Baptist into prison because John spoke the truth, and the king didn't want to hear it.

The Romans weren't the only ones who made life hard for the Jewish people. The Jewish religious leaders also put extra burdens on the people. The leaders added many picky, hard-to-follow rules to the Old Testament laws God had given the people. Many of these extra rules were about honoring the Sabbath. People who didn't follow the rules perfectly were treated as if they were unclean.

This was a very dark time, especially for the followers of God. But it was also at this exact time and place that God planned for Jesus to come to earth.

When God created the universe, He said, "Let there be light" (Genesis 1:3). Thousands of years later, He sent Jesus to earth as the "light of the world" (John

Loquacious Learning with Eugene

It's fascinating to me that human eyes are incapable of seeing the full spectrum (range) of light that exists in the world. Our eyes can detect a portion of the electromagnetic spectrum, including all of the colors of the rainbow. However, there are other types of light, such as ultraviolet and infrared light, that are invisible to the human eye. This makes *light* seem even more appropriate as a descriptive term for Christ: Some things we can see and understand about His character, and other things we can't. At least on this side of heaven.

8:12). In today's Bible passage, Jesus called Himself "a great light" (Matthew 4:16).

Jesus' light broke through the darkness and gave people life, hope, and truth. He had compassion on those who had been rejected by society. He healed the sick and brought the dead back to life. He gave sight to the blind and enabled the deaf to hear. He told stories about God's kingdom and His love. And He scolded some of the religious leaders for the way they treated people. Huge crowds followed Jesus from town to town because of the light and hope He brought.

Some people didn't like Jesus' light, probably because it showed wrong things in their lives that they wanted to hide. You may feel that way at times when God points out your sins. But if you ask Him, Jesus will shine His light into the dark corners of your life, and He'll forgive your sins!

Daily Challenge

Think back over your day. In what ways did you bring light into the world? Maybe you gave someone a compliment or a word of encouragement. Perhaps you volunteered to help your mom carry in the groceries without being asked. Or maybe you helped someone at school who tripped and dropped all of his or her books on the floor. Think about ways you can be even more of a light tomorrow.

Devo 9

Follow Me

Read Matthew 4:18–22.

Imagine you're out riding your bike, and a black limo pulls up beside you. The backseat window whirs down, and someone smiles at you. You do a double take. Is that *the president of the United States*? No, it couldn't be. But it is! You don't even know what to say when he looks at you and asks, "I'd like you to be my official secretary of state. How about it?"

That might have been how Peter and Andrew felt when Jesus called them to follow Him and become "fishers of men" (Matthew 4:19). And since they were fishermen, they most likely weren't very educated.[1] Yet this Teacher and Miracle Worker the entire town had been talking about was calling *them* to be His disciples!

They must have been thinking, *But we're fishermen. We smell bad. And besides, we don't know the Scriptures nearly as well as some other boys our age. Fishing is all we know! It's all we thought we'd ever do.*

But God had other plans for them. Bigger plans. These scrawny, dirty boys were probably content living simple fishermen's lives down by the docks, but Jesus saw something special in them. Peter would one day become the rock of Jesus' church (Matthew 16:18). John would become Jesus' best friend on earth (John 13:23). And Andrew would give up his life for the kingdom of God—as did the other two.[2] Their lives were too small when they met Jesus, but that was all about to change.

Jesus' disciples weren't like employees or students. They didn't go home at the end of the day or take weekends off. They walked wherever their Teacher, or

Wandering with Wooton

One time I ran across some baby ducks in the park who thought I was their mother. (I think they got confused because of the feathers on the hat I was wearing that day.) They started following me everywhere I went: up the seesaw, down the slide, under the jungle gym, around the tree. When I stopped to eat my lunch, they ate part of my sandwich. When I went fast, they sped up. When I swam across the lake, they were right behind me. Maybe that's what it's like to have disciples—people following you everywhere and trying to do everything you do. Talk about pressure! Thankfully I finally found the baby ducks' real mom, because—*whew!*—being a mother duck really builds up a sweat!

Rabbi, went, and they watched closely whatever He did. They slept where their Rabbi slept, ate their meals together, and engaged in long talks about the Old Testament with Him. By spending time with Jesus, these young men would grow to become just like Him. Like the disciples who followed Jesus two thousand years ago, we can be disciples of Jesus today. We can learn about God by reading the Bible and grow to be like Him.

Daily Challenge

Pray today that God will show you the plans He has for you, whenever the time is right. Give Him your dreams for the future one by one. Let Him know you trust that His plans for you are better than any you could make for yourself.

Devo 10

The Good News of the Day

Read Matthew 4:23–25.

Jesus was popular in His day. People followed Him everywhere. They left their homes and jobs to listen to Him preach. They brought Him their friends and family members who needed healing. They would even bring bedrolls and food and camp out so they could be near Him.

If the Internet had been invented in the first century, videos of Jesus would have been all over YouTube. Image what the news reports would have been like if they'd had TV:

NEWS REPORTER NELLY: I'm here in Galilee trying to see over the crowds. Jesus the Nazarene, whom all these thousands of people behind me came to see, will be starting His message shortly. In the meantime, I'll ask some of the crowd members why they're here. Excuse me, sir, what's your name and why are you here?

BRUCE: I'm Bruce, and I came because for the first time in thirty years, I can walk.

NEWS REPORTER NELLY: You used to be crippled?

BRUCE: I've been crippled since I was a baby. But I was lying on my mat one day begging, and Jesus came by with His disciples. All He did was talk to me. That's it. But His words were full of power. And then I felt this surge of strength in my legs. And I stood up . . .

NEWS REPORTER NELLY: That's amazing! So who are you here with?

BRUCE: I brought everyone I know who needs healing or is hurting in some way. This is Lucy. Her husband just died. And this is Marcus. He often has seizures. Peggy over there used to steal cows, but now she feels bad and wants forgiveness. Garrison came because he was curious. We carried Donna here on a stretcher because her fever is so high. The doctor said she's going to die, so this

Connie's Corner

When the freezer broke at Whit's End, Whit proclaimed it a free ice-cream day. You wouldn't believe how crowded this place was! People were driving all the way from Connellsville! Everyone was calling and e-mailing their friends to tell them about the deal. It was nuts! I guess good news travels fast. But it made me wonder what would happen if we were that excited about sharing Jesus with other people. What would the world be like?

is her last hope. Over there waving is Lawrence the Leper. No one wants to sit by him now because he's contagious and all, but that'll change pretty soon.

News Reporter Nelly: Wait, wait, wait! You think Jesus will heal *all* these people? And there are thousands of others. You really think He can somehow touch and heal each person?

Bruce: He came to heal and forgive and restore what's gone wrong. I know He can.

News Reporter Nelly: Anyone?

Bruce: Even you, Nelly. Have a seat . . . He's about to start!

The crowds following Jesus grew because He made such a big impact on people. That's why it's called the gospel or "good news"! If Jesus healed you the way He healed Bruce, wouldn't you be over-the-moon excited to tell your family, friends, and neighbors—even the bus driver?

Guess what? God *has* forgiven and saved you, given you a new heart, and promised you eternity in heaven with Him. Isn't that good news worth spreading, just as the crowds spread it in Jesus' day?

Daily Challenge

Think of someone you can share the good news of Jesus with. You don't have to recite a bunch of verses. Just share what Jesus has done in your life.

Devo 11

The Losers Win

Read Matthew 5:1–12.

Let's say you're at school, and you hear the following conversation in math class: "What's five plus five, Corey?"

"Ten, Mr. Platt."

"Nope, it's one hundred."

"That can't be! I learned those facts years ago. It's ten."

"Well, everything just changed. Now it's one hundred."

When Jesus gave His famous message called the Sermon on the Mount, the listeners must have thought He was as wrong as the math teacher, Mr. Platt. In today's Bible passage, Jesus turned everything on its head. *What? The meek will inherit the earth? That doesn't make sense. That's not what I've always thought!* The big difference between Jesus and Mr. Platt is that Jesus was speaking the truth!

Think about it: Usually the rich and powerful people in the world are the blessed ones. But look at verses 3–5 in Matthew 5. Take note of who is blessed: the poor in spirit, those who mourn, and the meek. These are people who have been wounded or are in need. They don't choose to be poor in spirit or meek or filled with grief. They become this way because of life's circumstances.

Notice that God speaks to them first. He doesn't just acknowledge them and give them a pat on the head; He *blesses* them! He promises good things out of the hard situations they endure. He fills them with the hope of heaven. He comforts them and fills them and promises to give them the earth.

God blesses those who need Him, and He blesses them by showing up. God knows what you need. He knows when you hurt. He knows when bullies make fun of you. He knows when you feel awful for making a bad choice and hurting

Whit's Wisdom

You might wonder how thousands of people could hear Jesus speak if He didn't use a megaphone or sound system like we have today. When I traveled to the Middle East, I actually visited the area where scholars think Jesus preached the Sermon on the Mount. I found it interesting that the way a steep hillside curves around the shoreline actually creates a natural amphitheater that makes sounds louder. Between eight and ten thousand people would have been able to hear Jesus speak in a normal voice!

someone else. He sees your needs, and He likes it when you bring them to Him. Because that's when you're open to hearing from Him.

In verses 7–12, Jesus promised more blessings for the merciful, the pure in heart, the peacemakers, and those who are insulted because they live godly lives. These people choose to be humble, wise, and gentle even though it's difficult. Jesus said that when people *choose* to be merciful and peaceful toward others, He will reward them. They are blessed.

"Blessed" is another way of saying happy or joyful. God wants you to have joy, but not the temporary kind you might get from a new game or a pocketful of money. He wants you to find your joy and happiness in Him. When you do, He'll give you the strength you need for difficult situations. And He'll give you the hope of better things to come!

Daily Challenge

Talk to your parents about some of the tough times they've been through and how God blessed them in the midst of them as they trusted Him.

Devo 12

A Salty Light

Read Matthew 5:13–16.

Here's an easy recipe for french fries. (If you want to make them, check with your mom first. The oil gets really hot.)

1. Cut a few baking potatoes lengthwise.
2. Fry in vegetable oil.
3. Eat plain.

And here are some directions for finding the hat you left outside:

1. Wait until it's completely dark.
2. Turn off any outside lights.
3. Go outside.
4. Find your hat.

Did you notice anything wrong with the recipe and directions? For one thing, fries don't taste good without salt. And it's hard to find things in the dark.

In today's Bible passage, Jesus first said, "You are the salt of the earth." A grain of salt is very small and common. Then He said, "You are the light of the world," which is something big and powerful. Why would He compare us to two things that are so different?

Let's take a closer look at salt.

Salt brings out the flavors of other foods. You probably wouldn't snack on spoonfuls of plain salt, but you'd like it sprinkled on other foods. Salt is in almost everything—from cakes and cookies to pizza and tacos. But you don't usually taste the salt in the food. You taste the other flavors the salt draws out. If you bit into something yummy, you probably wouldn't say, "Mmmm, I love the salt in this." Nope, you'd like the taste of the meat or the flavors of the sauce that the salt highlights.

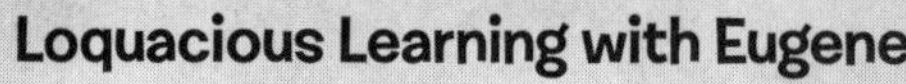

Loquacious Learning with Eugene

Centuries ago people believed that the moon produced its own light. Since then we've learned that the moon produces no light at all. It merely *reflects* the light of the sun as the two bodies align with each other. I remember looking out at a bright moon one night and considering that this is how we as believers reflect God's light to those around us. If we stay aligned with the Son of God, we can reflect *His* light. Even though people can't see God, they can still see us reflecting who He is.

Now think about light. If you enter a dark room and switch on a light, would you immediately look at the light? Probably not. The light itself isn't as important as what you're looking at in the room. The light helps you see furniture you need to walk around or a book you're looking for.

So even though salt and light are very different, they both cause us to notice other things.

Jesus said that His followers are salt and light in the world. That's because we draw people's attention to Him! They may notice that we act differently from others, or that we genuinely care about people. Or they might see the joy and hope we have and want to know what makes us different. That's when we can point them to the Savior. Just like a little salt on some good french fries!

Daily Challenge

Start using salt and light as reminders to live differently from others. When you bite into those fries in the cafeteria, remember that you represent Jesus and your language and actions around the lunch table should draw others to Him. Or when you turn on your light in the morning, think about things you can do during the day that will point people toward Jesus and make them want to know Him.

Devo 13

Rules, Rules, Rules

Read Matthew 5:17–20.

What if you were caught moving furniture around on a Sunday, and the punishment was being stoned to death? What if you weren't allowed to wear your favorite sweatshirt because it was made of two different kinds of material? Or what if you had to sacrifice a sheep every time you sinned so that God would forgive you?

As crazy as these rules sound, you would have had to obey them if you'd lived in Old Testament times (see Exodus 31:14; Leviticus 4:35; 19:19).

The religious leaders at that time added a bunch of rules to the laws God had given them through Moses. These extra instructions were called *hedge rules*, because like a hedge around a garden, they protected the true law of God. The hedge rules kept the people from even coming close to breaking the laws of God.[1] For example, God told His people to "remember the Sabbath day by keeping it holy" (Exodus 20:8). So the priests added hedge rules to make sure that happened. One of these rules said that the Jewish people weren't allowed to even *touch* a hammer on the Sabbath day because they might be tempted to use the hammer, which was work. And if they worked, they wouldn't be keeping the Sabbath holy.

Can you guess what happened? Yep . . . lots of additional rules were created, and it became more and more difficult for even good Jews to keep them all. Living a "holy" life became a burden, and that's not what God wanted for His people.

In today's Bible passage, Jesus reminded the people that God gave us His rules for our own good, not to make our lives difficult. God gave us rules because He loves us and wants to keep us safe. It's the same reason we have other kinds of rules. For example, you wouldn't let your dog eat chocolate because it would

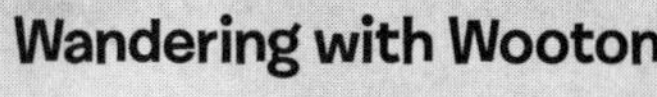

Wandering with Wooton

My mom wouldn't allow me to eat boysenberries when I was growing up. I thought it was really mean. I mean, all my friends could eat boysenberries! And those luscious berries looked really yummy! So one day I snuck outside, hid in some bushes down the street, and picked some. And then I ate them. Wow . . . they *were* really good! But then I noticed my ears were itching, and then my eyes began watering. I ran back home, and my mom said, "You ate boysenberries! You're allergic to boysenberries!" Sure enough, my face had swollen up to the size of a ceiling fan (or pretty close). One trip to the emergency room and twelve doses of medicine later, I understood the importance of rules!

make him sick. And parents put up baby gates to keep young children from falling downstairs or wandering into parts of the house where they could get hurt.

Some of the Jewish leaders thought Jesus was teaching that it wasn't important to obey the rules. But that wasn't what He meant at all! Jesus didn't come to throw away or destroy God's laws. He came to fulfill them and obey them all perfectly (Matthew 5:17).

We don't keep God's laws perfectly like Jesus did, but whenever we obey them, we show God that we love Him.

Daily Challenge

Go through the Ten Commandments with your family after dinner some night. Talk about how each commandment is for our benefit or protection. How do God's rules show you that He loves you?

Devo 14

The New Rules

Read Matthew 5:21-26; 43-48.

Abby folded her arms across her chest and narrowed her eyes. "What did you just say?" she asked the boy across the table.

The boy answered, "I said I'm sitting here now, so you'll have to find someplace else. Now get outta here!"

Abby felt the blood rush to her face. She wanted to hit that rude boy; he deserved it. She'd only gotten up for a minute, and he stole her seat, even though her friend had been saving it for her. The more she thought about it, the angrier she got. She clenched her fists and turned to walk away.

But she'd only walked a few steps when a police officer approached her. "Miss, I'm going to have to arrest you." He recited her legal rights as he tightened handcuffs around her wrists.

"But why?" she asked.

He yanked Abby outside toward a waiting police car. "For murder," the officer said. "You were having very angry thoughts."

Can you imagine if that really happened when we had angry thoughts? Everyone would be in jail!

In today's Bible passage, Jesus said it's not enough to make sure our actions are right. We need to make sure that our thoughts are right as well. God is much more interested in the condition of our hearts. Jesus taught that when we harbor angry thoughts toward others, it's as if we're committing murder!

Jesus' surprising words didn't end there. He went on to talk about loving our enemies. It's not enough to just tolerate them or ignore them. God wants us to *love* them!

Connie's Corner

The other day I got really mad at Penny, my roommate, for eating the piece of cake I'd left in the fridge. All day I was looking forward to eating it, but when I came home, it was gone. I knew Penny ate it, because she had frosting on her nose and a guilty look on her face! She didn't even ask me before eating it! I was so mad that I started thinking about how I could teach her a lesson. Maybe I'd wear her shoes without asking or eat the Pop-Tarts she put in the toaster. But then I realized how silly I was being. That wouldn't help our friendship at all. It would only make her mad at me, and what good would that do? So I decided to let it go. And next time, I'll label the package of cake "brussels sprouts."

Jesus came to show us God's extravagant love. It's easy to love people who are like us and treat us well. And most of us love people who are nice or good. But God's love is way bigger and more powerful than that. He even loved the people who arrested Him and killed Him!

In the *Odyssey* episode "Teacher's Pest" (album 41), Mandy finds herself in a dilemma. She is assigned to work on a science project with Max, the class troublemaker who sees it as his job to constantly mock Mandy. At first the two decide to simply split up the project so they won't have to work together. But Mandy eventually decides to reach out and be Max's friend. She even gives him a birthday present when no one else does. Mandy realizes that loving your enemy might just turn things around so you don't have an enemy at all!

Daily Challenge

Is there a bully in your neighborhood or at your school? Maybe it's someone who calls you names or laughs at you. Pray for that person today and think about how you can respond in love the next time he or she picks on you.

Word Scramble

Unscramble the letters in each puzzle to find the word clue. If you need help, use the Bible verse (NIV or NIRV) to guide you. Then write down all the numbered letters in corresponding order on the lines at the end. You'll find a famous saying of Jesus.

1. A son of Zebedee (Matthew 4:21)

M J S A E

___ ___ ___ ___ ___

1 2

2. The poor in spirit will find the kingdom of _____ (Matthew 5:3).

E H N A V E

___ ___ ___ ___ ___ ___

3 4

3. A Jewish "church," temple, or teaching place (Matthew 4:23)

N E Y G S O U A G

___ ___ ___ ___ ___ ___ ___ ___ ___

5 6 7

4. A book of the Old Testament that Jesus quoted from and that talks about "a great light" (Matthew 4:14-16)

A I H I S A

___ ___ ___ ___ ___ ___

8 9

Puzzle #2

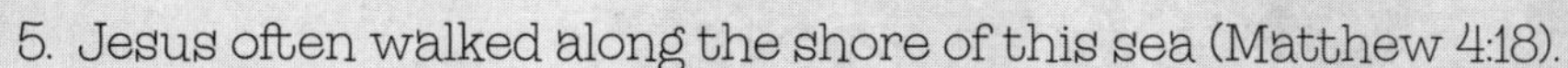

5. Jesus often walked along the shore of this sea (Matthew 4:18).

I L G E L E A

___ ___ ___ ___ ___ ___ ___

(10 under the 3rd blank, 11 under the 6th blank)

6. Peter's other first name (Matthew 4:18)

M S N O I

___ ___ ___ ___ ___

(12 under the 4th blank, 13 under the 5th blank)

7. Jesus left this city to go to Capernaum (Matthew 4:13).

Z T A H E A R N

___ ___ ___ ___ ___ ___ ___ ___

(14 under the 5th blank, 15 under the 6th blank)

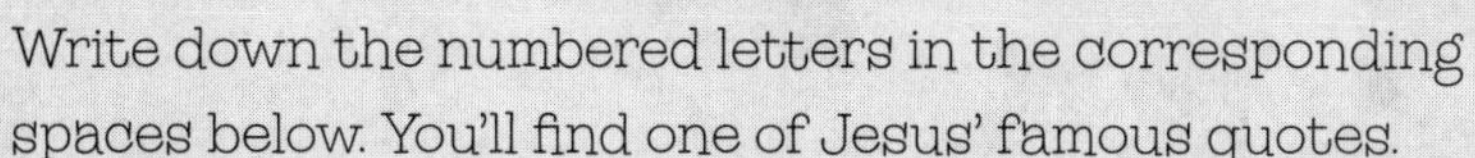

Write down the numbered letters in the corresponding spaces below. You'll find one of Jesus' famous quotes.

"___ ___ ___ ___   ___ ___ ___ ___

10 6 4 2   5 12 7 14

___ ___ ___ ___ ___ ___ ___" (Matthew 5:44)

3 13 15 1 9 11 8

Answers on page 209.

Devo 15

Shutting Off the Show-Off

Read Matthew 6:1-4; 16-18.

Imagine it's your birthday party, and you've just blown out the candles on the cake. Your parents bring out your present—a very large, oddly shaped object. You quickly unwrap it to find the new bike you'd been wanting!

But before you can even say thank you, your parents start telling everyone at the party all the trouble they went through to get it. For ten minutes your dad talks about how hard he had to work to earn the money. And your mom lists all the things she couldn't buy because they were saving up for it. Then they spend fifteen minutes talking about the time they spent driving to the store, finding the right bike, and fitting it in the car. Next they talk about the hassle of wrapping such an awkwardly shaped present. Half an hour later, the party guests pat your parents on the back. They praise your parents to the skies as you look at your bike. There's a lump of disappointment in your stomach as you realize you're no longer excited about it.

That's an example of how showing off takes away from the value of a gift. When you brag about the sacrifices you make for God, it tarnishes the gift. Or if you make sure everyone knows all the ways you help other people, it diminishes the gift. Instead of making the receiver feel special, it draws attention to the giver.

God wants you to give without showing off. In the *Odyssey* episode "Do, for a Change" (album 26), Eugene is happy to spout off all the information he has gained from his Bible studies and book reading. But he is more interested in impressing people than letting the Bible knowledge impact his heart. At the end of the episode, he finally learns to keep quiet about things.

Whit's Wisdom

Occasionally I fast. That is, I don't eat for a time so I can focus more completely on God. Going without eating sometimes makes me a little cranky, and once Connie said, "Whit, you're kind of irritable today. Are you fasting?" I had to chuckle, and I remembered today's Bible passage. Now I know that I should not only avoid looking haggard when I fast, but I should also make an effort to be more cheerful!

So whether you're putting money in the offering plate at church or picking up some trash in the school parking lot, don't make a big deal about it. God sees you even if no one else does. And His rewards are greater than anything you could receive here on earth.

Daily Challenge

Think of a way you could bless someone without the person knowing it's you. Maybe you could get up early to shovel the snow off a neighbor's driveway or clean up the kitchen for your mom while she's at the store. Don't expect credit or praise for what you're doing. Think of it as your gift to God!

Devo 16

The Model Prayer

Read Matthew 6:5–15.

Take this little true-or-false quiz:

1. True or false: To be a Christian, you must pray the Lord's Prayer every day.
2. True or false: The more times you say the Lord's Prayer each day, the more God will bless you.
3. True or false: You should pray outside and shout your prayers so that all your neighbors can hear you.

Of course the answers are *false*, *false*, and *false*. Jesus offered the Lord's Prayer as an example for His disciples to follow. He didn't mean for it to be the only prayer Christians pray. He doesn't want you to memorize it and recite it with no real feelings. And He certainly would frown if you were praying just to show off.

But the Lord's Prayer is an important model for Christians to follow, and it can help you learn to pray sincerely and effectively.

Our Father in heaven—The beginning of the Lord's Prayer is unique because it uses the word *Father*. When you pray, you don't need to start off with a lofty title for God. You can talk to Him in a very personal way. When you talk to your dad, you probably feel more freedom to say what's on your mind. Jesus was saying that we can approach God on a familiar level.

May your name be honored—Just because you have a personal relationship with God doesn't mean you should treat Him too casually, though. He's still God, and you should treat Him with respect. Jesus' prayer reminds us that God is holy and deserves our worship.

May your kingdom come. May what you want to happen be done on earth as it is done in heaven . . . Did you notice those pronouns? "*Your* kingdom," and "what

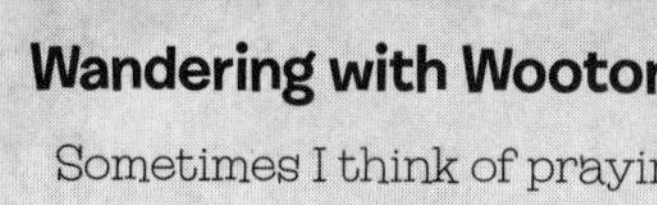

Wandering with Wooton

Sometimes I think of praying like making a sandwich. See, I make sandwiches differently every single time. Sometimes I put in salami or pickles or peanuts or cheese or whipped cream. Sometimes I put all of them on the bread, and sometimes I use different combinations. But I always like to surround everything with two pieces of bread. My prayers are kind of a variety too. Sometimes I have a *lot* of things to ask God to forgive me for. Other times I thank Him for things but mix it up with a few requests, too. But I always surround my prayers with two things. I start with "Hi, Father in heaven. You're awesome!" and end with "Thanks for being so great. Amen."

you want to happen." Jesus reminded His disciples (and us!) that praying isn't about telling God our plans and expecting Him to make them happen. It's about inviting God to work in the way He thinks is best, because *He* knows best, not us.

Give us today our daily bread—God knows your needs. In this verse, Jesus was showing us a way to say, "I'm looking to You to take care of me today, God."

Forgive us our sins, just as we also have forgiven those who sin against us—If you've received the gift of God's forgiveness by trusting in Jesus, you now have the freedom and responsibility to forgive people who have wronged you.

Keep us from falling into sin when we are tempted. Save us from the evil one—Notice that Jesus said *when* we are tempted, not *if*. Temptations and troubles are bound to come into your life. But you're not alone in fighting them off. God is always there to help you.

Daily Challenge

Write out the Lord's Prayer in your own words. Include all those aspects Jesus talked about: expressing a close relationship with God, showing Him respect, asking for His will to be done, sharing your concerns and needs, asking Him to forgive you (and those who hurt you), and asking for His guidance and protection as you try to live a life that pleases Him.

Devo 17

Who's Your Master?

Read Matthew 6:19–24.

Ask your friends what they'd like that would make them happy. You'll probably hear responses like "a new movie," "a skateboard," or "an iPod." But a recent study showed that the people who are often the happiest in life are those who have strong relationships with friends and family, have attitudes of thankfulness, and have a "spiritual connection."[1]

Isn't it interesting that people in the survey said they'd be happy if they had things that cost money? But what *actually* makes people happy are things that don't cost a penny!

The desire for more money isn't anything new. The Bible has hundreds of verses related to money, wealth, and spending; some Bible scholars claim more than a thousand.[2] That's more than verses about prayer or heaven or even salvation! Money must have been a pretty hot topic in Bible times. And it's still a hot topic today!

In today's Bible passage, Jesus wasn't saying we shouldn't have money. Money is important for living and saving and giving. We need money to eat and to have a place to live, for example. And we need to save money for things like college or to open a business someday. But money becomes a problem when it's more important to us than serving God. We know it's getting control over us when we start making bad decisions, such as. . .

"I know I got too much change back from the sales clerk, but I want the money. I'm not going to give it back. It's the clerk's fault anyway."

Or . . . "I'm not going to give money to church this week because I really want to save up for a new skateboard."

Or . . . "I really want the new boots everyone else is getting, so I think all the

Loquacious Learning with Eugene

I've realized recently that I spend a significant percentage of my income on technology and media. It could be anything from a new gadget to a magazine subscription. My wife, Katrina, challenged me to take a month and purchase only the items I actually needed. Of course I accepted the challenge posthaste. I quickly realized that many of the items I thought I needed weren't necessarily, well, necessary. With the extra money I'd saved by the end of the month, we were able to send a check to some missionaries in Africa. And I must admit that felt even better than acquiring the latest gadget!

time about how I can get them and how great life will be once I have them."

Have you ever made decisions like that? Does money (or the stuff it buys) control you? Is it your master?

In the *Odyssey* episode "Treasures of the Heart" (album 16), Jimmy Barclay wants to spend all his money on a new pair of shoes, just because they are the cool shoes to have at his school. The shoes become more important to him than making wise choices.

God has given you things so you can *enjoy* them, not so they can control you. Jesus tells us to "store up for yourselves treasures in heaven" (Matthew 6:20). Everything you buy here on earth will be destroyed someday. Your skateboard will eventually break, and your boots will fall apart. But the time, energy, and money you spend doing God's work will have results that last forever!

Daily Challenge

Keep a jar in your room, and give part of your allowance, or whatever you earn, to a cause you believe in. Pray about how God wants you to give—maybe supporting the local homeless shelter, sponsoring a child in another country, or making a special offering at church.

Devo 18

No Worries

Read Matthew 6:25-34.

"I'm afraid I'm going to fail my math test."

"Everybody's going to laugh at me."

"I'm never going to have any friends."

"I'm so nervous about my report card. My parents are going to be so mad."

"What if I strike out? What if we lose the game, and it's all my fault?"

"Grandpa's really sick . . . What if he dies?"

Do any of these worries sound familiar? We all have things we're concerned about. In the *Odyssey* episode "Our Daily Bread" (album 17), the Barclays worried because Mr. Barclay lost his job. The loss affected the whole family. But Jesus tells us three times in today's Bible passage, "Do not worry. . . Do not worry. . . Do not worry." Go back through the passage and underline that phrase. When Jesus repeats something, it's especially important.

Jesus also tells us to think about birds and lilies and remember how God cares for them. Think about that for a minute. God provides food and shelter for the tiniest of birds. He even crafts flower petals and provides dew for the flowers that *no one ever sees*. Then Jesus asked His followers, "Are you not much more valuable than they?" (Matthew 6:26). Yes, yes! A thousand times yes! Your Father in heaven cares for you a million times more than He cares for the birds or the lilies. Surely since He watches over them, He'll watch even more closely and carefully over you!

God knows your needs, and He even knows your heart. He's well aware of what you're worried about, what hurts you, and what you want. That's no mystery to Him. But just because He knows all about you, it doesn't mean things will always go your way. Disappointments will still happen. You might not make the

Connie's Corner

I have a horrible fear of staplers. No, really, I do. I know it's weird, and I know it's crazy. But I jump every time I hear one, like I'm afraid it's going to come after me and staple my ears to my elbows or something. Wooton is afraid of hurting people, Eugene is afraid of needles, and Penny is afraid of getting hit by a cement truck. Everyone has fears, I guess. The important thing to remember is that God is bigger than any of them.

team, for example. Or you might get laughed at. Or Grandpa might pass away. But you can know for sure that God sees your hurts, knows about your concerns, and will provide what you need. So give all your worries and fears to Him!

Daily Challenge

Think about what fears and worries you have today. Close your eyes and imagine taking each concern and putting it in God's outstretched hand so He can take care of it. Thank Him that He cares so much about you.

Devo 19

Where Did I Put That Plank?

Read Matthew 7:1–6.

What would you think if you saw this happen at the local swimming pool? A girl jumps into the pool. She surfaces, sputtering.

The lifeguard says, “Why did you jump into the pool if you can’t swim?”

The girl is flailing in the water, but she manages to shout, “I don’t know!”

“It’s really not very bright of you,” the lifeguard lectures her. “You should think things through next time.”

“You’re right,” she says, coughing. “You’re right . . .”

“Okay, I’ll come get you.” Then he jumps into the water.

A moment later, he surfaces, sputtering and coughing.

“Are you okay?” she asked.

“No!” the lifeguard says. “I can’t swim either!”

This is a silly story, but it illustrates what Jesus is telling us in today’s Bible passage. Sometimes it’s easy to see other people’s shortcomings without noticing our own. Our flaws might not seem as big as the flaws of other people we know. But think about this: Have you ever resented someone for losing his or her temper with you? Anger is a sin, but so is bitterness. Or have you whispered to your friends about the girl who got caught shoplifting? Gossip and stealing are sins too.

The Bible tells us in Romans 3:23 that “all have sinned and fall short of the glory of God.” We’re *all* sinners. We’ve all made mistakes. And we first need to look at our own lives to see where we need to grow and what sins we need to confess.

It doesn’t mean we don’t tell our friends when we think what they’re doing is wrong, but we need to have a humble attitude about it. We’re not any better than

Loquacious Learning with Eugene

According to my bedtime reading of *Strong's Exhaustive Concordance*, the Greek word for "hypocrite" used in verse 5 is the same word that is used for "actor."[1] In other words, Jesus was saying that those who judge others without looking at their own flaws are like actors. They are pretending to be someone they're not.

they are. So the next time you have a fight with a friend, and he or she says some mean things to you, first apologize for the mean things you said to your friend. Or the bad attitude you had. Or ask forgiveness for being too proud to admit *you* were wrong. *Then* you can tell your friend how hurt you feel.

Daily Challenge

Ask a parent or a friend you trust to point out some of the areas in your life where you need to grow. Pay attention to what your parent or friend says, and respond graciously.

Devo 20

The Snake Rule

Read Matthew 7:7–12.

At the local fast-food drive-through:*

"Welcome to Fishy Town. May I take your order?" says the voice through the speaker.

"Yeah, can I get the fish and . . . um . . . some bread, please?" says the driver.

"All right, that's a snake with a side of rocks. Would you like that snake with tomato or onions?"

"I didn't ask for a snake. Or rocks. I asked for fish and bread."

"I understand. And how would you like that snake cooked? Well done or rare?"

"Why would I eat a snake?"

"And would you like those rocks as pebbles, or should I supersize them to boulders?"

In today's Bible reading, Jesus asked the question, "If your child asks for bread, would you give him a stone?" (Matthew 7:9, paraphrase). Of course not. Children aren't supposed to eat rocks. A parent would give a child what he or she needs. God wants to give us what we need too. He loves us and wants what's best for us. So He tells us to ask Him for whatever we need. Remember that God won't necessarily give us everything we *want*, but He will supply all of our *needs* (Philippians 4:19).

Just as God meets our needs, we should try to help others. For example, if you saw a boy getting picked on by a bully, would you walk away or try to help him? What would you want someone to do for you? Helping others is called the Golden Rule: "Do to others what you would have them do to you" (Matthew 7:12).

Connie's Corner

Once, as a joke, I hung a geeky picture of ten-year-old Eugene on the bulletin board at Whit's End. I knew Eugene hated the picture, but I thought it was funny. Then Whit found out and handed me a yardstick that he had painted gold. He said, "Make sure you hang the picture up straight." I said, "What is this?" He said, "It's my golden ruler." It was his way of telling me to treat others the way I want to be treated. I took down the picture.

The opposite is true too: Don't do to others what you wouldn't want them to do to you! Do you like being teased? Do you like it when people lie to you? How about when your little brother eats fourteen of Mom's fresh-baked cookies and leaves none for you? Do you like that? Of course not! So don't do those kinds of things to others. The Golden Rule is a great rule to live by.

Another rule: Don't go to Fishy Town. They overcook their snake meat.

Daily Challenge

Do something unexpectedly nice for someone and watch his or her reaction. If the person does something nice back, you've just seen the Golden Rule passed forward. If not, at least you made someone happy for a few moments.

Devo 21

A Tight Squeeze

Read Matthew 7:13–14.

In a famous series of experiments, a bunch of people were placed in a room together. They were shown three lines and were asked which line was the longest. The middle line was clearly the longest. But all of the people except one were told beforehand to say aloud that the third line was the longest. One person wasn't told to say anything. This experiment was done a number of times, and more than seven out of ten times, the uninformed person went along with the crowd and said that the last line was the longest, even though it wasn't.[1]

Why do people go along with the crowd even when they know it's wrong?

Have you ever pleaded with your parents to buy you something because "Everyone else has one"? Have your parents ever responded, "If everyone else jumped off a cliff, would you do it too?" Guess what? Your parents may need an updated example, but they're right. "Everyone" is sometimes wrong.

Often, God's way isn't the same as the crowd's way. The crowd tells us to make ourselves happy. God tells us to put the concerns of others first. The crowd tells us to get revenge. God tells us to forgive. In today's Bible passage, Jesus called this the "narrow gate" (Matthew 7:13) because it's a harder path to take than the wide way. It's hard to live by God's rules. It's hard to go against the crowd. We want to fit in. We want people to love us, so we try to be like them. How much better would it be if we tried instead to be like Jesus?

It's a tight squeeze to get through that narrow passageway. But there are rewards when we do things God's way. Jesus said that the narrow road "leads to life" (verse 14), but the wide road "leads to destruction" (verse 13). Or off a cliff! Which road would you rather take?

Wandering with Wooton

One time I got lost on my mail route and somehow ended up in this building where everyone had canes in their hands. I figured canes were back in fashion, like in the 1920s when everybody had canes and wore black top hats. I didn't want to be the only one left out of the fun, so I grabbed a cane and walked around with it too. Then I saw the sign that said School for the Blind. I had to return the cane. Giving in to peer pressure can be so embarrassing!

Daily Challenge

Go against the crowd today. Sit next to a lonely kid at lunch instead of a big group. Shut down a piece of gossip or a joke you know is hurtful or wrong. Or be the one to say no when your friends decide to do something they shouldn't be doing.

Bible Code

Find the rest of the letters in the Bible passage on the next page, which was taken from the book of Matthew. The grid is your code box. Figure out the rest of the letters of the code, and you'll be able to finish the verse.

Hint: You have to guess at the letters from the verse and figure the code out by trial and error. Can you guess which word in the verse is DO? What number is O? We've done one word for you (give). (If you get stuck, see Matthew 7:6.)

A	B	C	D	E	F	G	H	I	J	K	L	M
				2		8		6				

N	O	P	Q	R	S	T	U	V	W	X	Y	Z
								9				

						G	I	V	E				
___	___	___	___	___		___	___	___	___	___	___	___	___
11	4	21	4	20		8	6	9	2	11	4	8	10

25 15 14 20   6 10   10 14 18 26 2 11;

11 4   21 4 20   20 15 26 4 25

13 4 19 26   17 2 14 26 16 10

20 4   17 6 8 10.

Answer on page 209.

Devo 22

Deadly Disguise

Read Matthew 7:15–20.

Who wouldn't want a puffer fish in their home aquarium? They're so adorable! The puffer fish is also called a blowfish. It's the one in the movie *Finding Nemo* that blows up like a balloon. How can you possibly keep from giggling when those goofy-looking cheeks get all puffy?

Of course, they stop being so adorable if you eat one. Puffer fish contain a poison called tetrodotoxin, which paralyzes your muscles. There is no cure for tetrodotoxin. If you get a nice big dose of this poison, it paralyzes your diaphragm. Your diaphragm helps you breathe. So you'll end up suffocating under the weight of your own chest.[1]

Are you still giggling?

There are a lot of cute, fun, and exciting things that can also harm us. In today's Bible passage, Jesus warns us of people who are like this. Throughout your life, you'll meet people who seem wise and interesting but are really telling you lies. Jesus calls them "false prophets" (Matthew 7:15). He tells us to beware of these people because they're like wolves dressed up as sheep. They look harmless on the outside, but underneath they're really dangerous.

How can you tell the difference between the truth and a lie? First, you have to know the truth. You can learn what the truth is by reading the Bible every day. Second, if someone says something that doesn't line up with the teachings of the Bible, it's wrong. Period. At some point in your life, interesting and attractive people may tell you that Jesus wasn't God's Son. They may say that Jesus never really existed, never died on the cross, and never rose from the dead. They're false prophets because what they're teaching is different from what the Bible teaches.

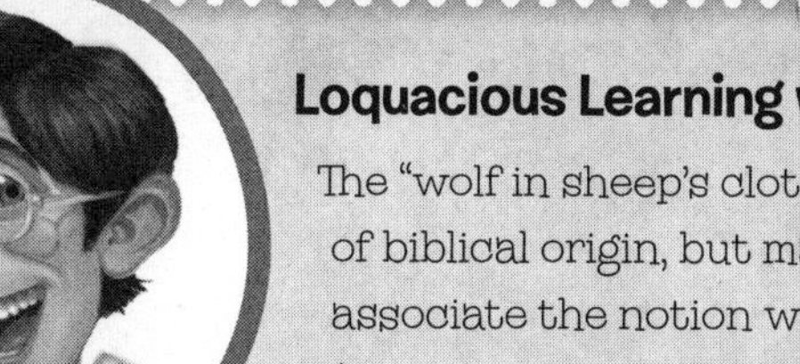

Loquacious Learning with Eugene

The "wolf in sheep's clothing" metaphor is of biblical origin, but many experts also associate the notion with *Aesop's Fables*. Aesop was an ancient storyteller who is believed to have lived in ancient Greece. In one of Aesop's stories, a wolf disguised itself as a sheep to deceive the flock. The gullible sheep trusted the wolf, and the wolf eventually enjoyed a hearty meal of tasty mutton (sheep meat). The lesson of Aesop's story is similar to Jesus' warning to His disciples: Appearances can be deceptive.

When Jesus talked about these people, He said twice, "By their fruit you will recognize them" (verses 16, 20). The fruit Jesus was talking about is a person's actions. We need to watch what people do more than what they say. Some people produce good fruit (actions) in their lives, and some produce rotten fruit. If their actions don't follow the Bible, don't trust the things that come out of their mouths!

Daily Challenge

The next time you watch television or read something on the Internet that you think might be wrong, ask your parents to help you find a Bible verse that explains why it's wrong. Sometimes there's not a specific verse that deals exactly with what you're asking (the words "cell phone," for example, aren't in the Bible), but there are almost always general principles about how to treat others, which are explained clearly.

Devo 23

Solid as a Rock

Read Matthew 7:24–29.

Have you and your friends ever built a human pyramid? If there are six of you, you put three people on their hands and knees on the bottom row. Then two people climb onto the backs of the people on the bottom and balance on their hands and knees. Finally, one person climbs on top of the pyramid and balances on his or her hands and knees.

What's the key thing to remember when you build a human pyramid? Don't put a four-year-old kid on the bottom row, where he has to support a two-hundred-fifty-pound football player. To build a really good human pyramid, you have to put the strong, big kids on the bottom and the smaller kids on the top. Otherwise, you're going to have a tangled mess of bodies on the floor . . . and maybe even some injuries. (That four-year-old kid might just get squashed!)

Like building a human pyramid, if you want to build a tall tower, you need a solid foundation. The most important thing is making sure the bottom part of the tower is strong. Jesus talked about this in today's Bible passage when He said, "Everyone who hears these words of mine and puts them into practice is like a wise man who built his house on the rock" (Matthew 7:24). Before you can grow stronger and wiser as a Christian, you must first build a solid foundation by trusting Jesus and obeying His teachings.

It's tempting to take shortcuts in life. The man who built his house on the sand in Jesus' parable was taking a shortcut. He didn't build his house on a solid foundation, and he ended up getting swept away by the wind and rain.

In the same way, if you don't take the time to grow in your faith and learn

Whit's Wisdom

Do you know why the Tower of Pisa leans? Because the builders mistakenly constructed the 183-foot-tall marble building on top of a dense clay mixture that sunk unevenly over time. It wasn't built on solid ground. Over the next eight hundred years, people tried to fix the tower in various ways, but all attempts failed until recently when an eight-year-long project succeeded in "de-tilting" the tower by fifteen inches.[1]

If you ever find yourself leaning or drifting further away from God, go back to the solid foundation–the Bible and the teachings of Jesus. That's the best foundation for the choices you make in life.

how to follow Jesus, you can get swept away by all sorts of things. So many things in this world can get in your way and keep you from becoming a loyal follower of Jesus. Television can teach you the wrong things. Friends can convince you to do the wrong things. Magazines and the Internet can give you bad advice.

But if you study the Bible and trust Jesus, you can build a solid foundation that won't crumble when life gets stormy.

Daily Challenge

Now that you've finished the Sermon on the Mount (Matthew chapters 5–7), go back and read it again all at once. These lessons are directly from Jesus, and they can help you build a rock-solid foundation for your life.

Devo 24

Everyday Miracles

Read Matthew 8:1–17.

Today's Bible passage begins a series of events where Jesus did miraculous things. When Jesus was on earth, He had power over the weather, over demons, and over sickness. You may wonder if Jesus still has this power today. If so, you're not the only one.

In the *Odyssey* episode "Run-of-the-Mill Miracle" (album 48), Grady McKay's sister, Samantha, wound up in the hospital because of carbon monoxide poisoning. The doctors were worried that she might not survive, and Grady was worried too. He prayed and asked God, "Please make my sister wake up and be okay . . . please."

Next, Grady got into the Imagination Station and traveled to Bible times. He witnessed Jesus healing a boy from ten miles away. Then he watched Elijah feed a poor widow with a jar of flour and a jar of oil that filled up on their own!

Grady understood that God did these miracles, but they happened so long ago. So Grady asked Whit, "How come God can't do that now?"

Whit explained that miracles happen a lot: "Maybe the really big ones don't seem to happen as often, but God works small miracles all the time." He suggested that Grady talk to Joanne Allen. Joanne told Grady how she drove up a snowy mountain at night to help a woman who was having a baby. When Joanne drove down the mountain the next morning, she discovered by the light of day that there was no way she could have come up that mountain road without an angel holding the car on the road. The road was too narrow!

Things that humans can't explain happen all the time. Have you ever heard stories about people who were miraculously healed even after doctors said there

Connie's Corner

I've learned to appreciate the little miracles in my life. The other day, I lost my wallet. It had my license, my bank cards, my money, my *life*! I was freaked out, but then I took some time to pray. It calmed me down, and two hours later, when I wasn't even looking for it, I found my wallet wedged between the washer and dryer! What would even make me look there? It was a small miracle. Okay, not exactly the parting of the Red Sea, but I do believe that God does amazing things for those who are looking to Him for help.

was no chance for them to live? Or someone escaping a car accident unharmed when the car was completely destroyed? Or someone deciding to send money to a missionary, and it just happened to be the *exact* amount the missionary needed to buy medicine? God still does miracles. He doesn't do them all the time, but when He does, it should remind us that He has power over everything in our world—and beyond.

Daily Challenge

With your parents' permission, do some research on the Internet or in books about missionaries and find stories about how God worked miracles in people's lives. Ask your parents to help you and make it a family project!

Devo 25

In the Middle of a Storm

Read Matthew 8:23–27.

Waves crashed against the boat, knocking Peter down to the deck. John, who was drenched to the skin, clung to the mast as the winds howled overhead. Andrew threw things overboard in hopes of keeping the struggling boat afloat.

"It's getting worse!" shouted John over a roar of thunder. "We can't steer anymore." The boat tipped dangerously in the water, and a surge of water rushed over the side.

"Where's Jesus?" called Peter.

"By the stern," Andrew answered. "Go get Him!"

A disciple headed to the stern to find his Master sleeping peacefully. What? How could He be *sleeping* through this storm? Peter shook him awake. "Jesus! Jesus! Save us! We're going to drown!"

Do you ever feel like the disciples did that stormy night on the Sea of Galilee? Have you gone through struggles when you wondered if God was sleeping? When life feels chaotic or out of control, do you wonder whether He even cares?

How did Jesus respond to His disciples that night on the stormy sea? He said, "Your faith is so small! Why are you so afraid?" (Matthew 8:26, NIRV).

Think about it: The disciples had just witnessed Jesus doing many, many miracles. Yet they came to Him in a panic. "We're going to drown!" they cried (verse 25). Do you wonder what they were thinking? *Sure, Jesus can do miracles. But this is too big for Him. Or maybe He'll help others out, but for some reason He won't help us.*

It's easy to have faith when we're not in the midst of a struggle. We can say we believe that Jesus will help us, but when the waves start crashing over the sides

Whit's Wisdom

A huge storm hit Odyssey a few years back. It was so strong, it blew in the window at Whit's End, and shards of glass wounded my leg. While Connie ran for help, I quoted the Psalms aloud–both as a prayer to God and as a reminder that even in the midst of scary situations, God is still in control.

of the boat, it's harder to hold on to our faith. Just because Jesus is in your life doesn't mean that storms won't come along. Being a Christian doesn't mean that life will be easy. But it does mean you always have Someone to turn to for help. He can calm the storms or keep you safe in the middle of them.

Daily Challenge

List ways God has provided for you in the past. Or jot down a few stories you've heard from other people about how He's cared for them. God is faithful. He's not going to abandon you. Remember that no matter what your storm is right now, God is taking care of you.

Devo 26

Victory . . . with a Side of Bacon

Read Matthew 8:28–34.

School shootings. Robberies. Wars. Cancer. Road rage. Prisons. Bullies. We know there is evil and sickness in this world. We only need to watch the news or read a newspaper to see that bad things happen every day. People are hurt. People sin. Tragedies happen. That's the bad news.

But here's the good news: Jesus tells us in John 16:33, "Take heart! I have overcome the world." This isn't the Super Bowl competition, where the outcome is uncertain beforehand. The victory has already been won. We know the outcome. But the battle is still playing out. Temptation, evil, and darkness are battling against light, hope, and redemption.

Even when it seems like the devil's winning, God has something else up His sleeve. Remember some of these events?

- The earth was flooded . . . *but* God repopulated the world and gave humans a new promise (Genesis 6–9).
- Joseph's brothers sold him into slavery . . . *but* God used his time in Egypt to bring him to a place of authority and save lives (Genesis 37:23–28).
- The Egyptians made the Jewish people serve them as slaves . . . *but* God sent Moses to rescue them (Exodus 3–4).
- The Red Sea blocked the way of escape when the Israelites were fleeing from Pharaoh's army . . . *but* God divided the sea so they could walk through on dry land (Exodus 14).
- The walls of Jericho were strong and tall . . . *but* God made them fall anyway (Joshua 6).

Connie's Corner

I think God has created each of us with the knowledge in our hearts that good will win in the end. That's why we like stories with happy endings. We want evil to be stopped and the good guys to succeed. We want the princess to be rescued, the underdog to win, and the weeping mother to find her missing child. It's funny to me that whether Hollywood producers believe in God or not, their movies tell the gospel story over and over. Good conquers evil.

Sometimes it might feel as if evil is winning. But it isn't. A day is coming when Jesus will send evil back where it belongs, just as He sent those evil spirits and pigs into the sea in today's Bible passage.

Daily Challenge

As you hear about tragedies on the news, instead of growing worried about them, stop and pray instead. Read a newspaper and pray for the people whose lives have been broken by tragedy. Ask God to turn the situation around for good, so that He will be glorified through it.

Devo 27

First Things First

Read Matthew 9:1–8.

It's so simple, Greg. I know you can do it without me there," Mom said over the phone.

"Okay, tell me how to bake the cookies. I have the yellow tube of dough right here." Greg flipped it over in his hand.

"Good. All you have to do is slice the dough with a knife, place the slices on a cookie sheet, and bake the cookies for ten minutes at 350 degrees."

Greg jotted down the instructions, thanked his mom, and then got to work.

Twenty minutes later, Mom returned from the grocery store. As she opened the door, she smelled a terrible odor.

"Ew! What happened?" she asked. "It smells awful in here!"

"It's the cookies," Greg said. "And they taste even worse than they smell."

Mom looked at the stove, where the cookies sat cooling on a cookie sheet.

Greg said, "I did everything you said, Mom. I don't know why they didn't turn out."

Mom could see that Greg had done everything she told him to do, but she hadn't included one important step in her instructions.

"Greg, dear," she said, laughing, "you were supposed to take the cookies *out of the package* before you sliced and baked them!"

Sometimes if you miss the first step of the instructions, nothing else works out. Like writing a book before you learn how to read. Or trying to catch a fish but forgetting to bring a fishing pole.

In today's Bible passage, Jesus reminds us about the importance of the first

Wandering with Wooton

So, the other day I was delivering mail when I saw this elderly chipmunk that kinda looked like my Aunt Edna. Same furrowed eyebrows and fuzzy nose. Same big teeth and tendency to chew with her mouth open. And then it hit me. Aunt Edna's birthday was last week! I missed it! I hurried home to call her and sing my special happy birthday song, but first I knew I needed to apologize for forgetting about her birthday. Sometimes the "I'm sorry" needs to come first. You know, maybe I shouldn't have told you this story. I guess on my next phone call, I'll have to say I'm sorry for comparing her to an elderly chipmunk.

step of being made right with Him: asking Jesus to forgive our sins. When the paralyzed man's friends brought him to Jesus, his hope was that Jesus could heal him. But the first thing Jesus said was "Your sins are forgiven" (Matthew 9:2).

We often come to Jesus with a whole list of needs and wants. These things matter to Him, but what matters most is our hearts. God is more concerned with the condition of your heart than your circumstances. He wants you to be right with Him before anything else in your life is made "right." First, Jesus forgave the paralyzed man, *then* He healed the man's body and sent him off to celebrate at home with his family.

Daily Challenge

The next time you kneel down to ask Jesus for something, also ask Him to examine your heart. Is there any sin (wrong thoughts or actions) in your life that you need to tell God about and ask His forgiveness for? Is there someone you need to apologize to? Is God reminding you of something you should do but have been putting off? Think about these things *first*.

Devo 28

Dr. Jesus

Read Matthew 9:9–13.

The doctor entered the waiting room and said, "I'm ready for my first patient." Nurse Nancy handed him a clipboard. "Mr. Green is first," she replied. "He has a cold."

"Ooh." Concern was etched on the doctor's face. "I don't want to see him. He'll probably sneeze on me."

Nurse Nancy handed him another clipboard. She asked, "How about Mrs. Carter, then? She has a rash."

"She might be contagious," he whispered in the nurse's ear. "I don't want to catch anything."

Nurse Nancy continued to go through the list of the day's patients. A stomach bug. A toenail fungus. The doctor dismissed them all.

Finally he turned to her and asked, "Can't I see someone who's *healthy*?"

It's a good thing Jesus wasn't like that doctor! In today's Bible passage, Jesus said, "Those who are healthy don't need a doctor. Sick people do" (Matthew 9:12, NIRV).

The religious leaders of Jesus' day were concerned about the company Jesus was keeping. Why was He hanging out with sinners? Take that awful tax collector, Matthew, for example. Everyone knew he was a cheat and a swindler. After all, if Jesus really had been sent from God as He claimed to be, then He should have been hanging out with better people. People like the religious leaders who spent long hours at the synagogue, knew the laws of God, and obeyed them.

But Jesus wasn't interested in hanging out with the people who thought they

Connie's Corner

When I first started learning about Jesus, I didn't have the mind of a Christian yet. I was pretty stubborn and thought I had life all figured out. And because I was stubborn, I was sometimes judgmental and too critical toward other people. I'd argue a lot with Eugene or complain about the silliest things. But God knew what I was going through and how I needed to grow. He didn't wait for me to be perfect before He started working on me. Through Whit and others, God showed His care for me. And as I recognized His unconditional love for me, I fell in love with Him. I'm so, so, so thankful God doesn't ignore us when we're messed up.

had it all together. Over and over He chose to socialize with the people who *knew* they needed Him. They weren't out to impress Jesus. They knew they were broken and trapped in their sin. And they knew Jesus could help them.

Daily Challenge

Skim through your Bible to find some imperfect people God used. It's not hard. He seems to like people who have questionable histories or flawed personalities as we learned in Devo 1. (Maybe because these people are the ones who need Him the most!) Then interview your youth pastor, your Sunday school teacher, and your senior pastor about mistakes they've made. Ask each one how God turned him or her around.

Bible Basics Code

Jesus reminds us that before a person can grow stronger and wiser as a Christian, he or she must first believe and follow His basic teachings.

Starting at the shaded E, follow the directions that are below the next dash to fill in the next letter. L means "letter to the left." R means "letter to the right." U means "letter that is up or above." D means "letter that is down or underneath." For example, the directions to the right of the E say "L2." That means, starting from the E in the code box, you would move two spaces to the left, which leads you to the letter V. From the V, you would move three spaces up to the E. And so on.

When you're done, you'll find out what Jesus told the crowds in Matthew 7:24. (Hint: It's about the importance of having a solid spiritual foundation.)

Z	S	R	L	E	T	K	P
R	H	E	T	U	I	S	W
Y	U	N	I	O	M	I	K
E	R	D	H	P	A	R	N
S	B	V	O	**E**	H	T	C
R	O	S	P	W	F	L	H
A	H	I	C	M	E	N	E
H	O	T	X	A	D	C	N

E ___ ___ ___ ___ ___ ___ ___   ___ ___ ___
(blank) L2 U3 L2 D1 R4 L2 U1   R5 D4 L6

D1 R4 U3 R1 U2   L3 D2 L3 D1 R4

D1 L3 U2 R1 D2   L1 R4   U3 R1 D4 L1

U3 R2 L5   R2 U2 L1 R3   D3 L1 D2 U4

R1 D4 U2 L3   D1 L3 D1 R3 U5 D1 D4 R2

L3 U1   R4 U3 R1 D4   L7   R4 D1 R3

U6 D4 L6   U1 U2 R2 U2 R2   D4 U3 R1

L5 D4 U3 U2 R3   D2 L2   D5 L2 U4

R1 D4 R5 U7.

Answer on page 209.

Devo 29

Doing Things Differently

Read Matthew 9:14–17.

You just had a really, really bad day.

Your dog died, you flunked your math test, and you got a terrible haircut and now have a bald spot over your left ear. To top if off, you got food poisoning from the school cafeteria's tater tots and have been feeling nauseated all day. Good thing your best friend is coming over to cheer you up.

But today she shows up with a list. *Huh...that's strange,* you think.

You see that it is a whole typed list of things to do.

She gives you a hug. Then she checks off a box on her sheet. She smiles at you. Then she checks off another box. "I'm so sorry you had a bad day," she reads off the sheet. Then she checks it off. She offers a few more phrases from her sheet, but they're not very helpful. When she gets up to leave, she tells you she will call you later that day. She checks her paperwork, then corrects herself. "I'll call you twice, and I'll send you a card." She leaves as suddenly as she came, but somehow, you don't feel any better.

This is how the Pharisees often related to God. They were really good at following the rules and checking all the boxes. Praying? Check. Fasting? Check. Spending hours at the temple? Check. They thought they were pretty good at being godly people.

But Jesus had something else in mind. He wants a relationship with His followers, not just a to-do list for them to accomplish. That's why Jesus said you had to use new wineskins. The old wineskin—the to-do list—had to be replaced with a new attitude.

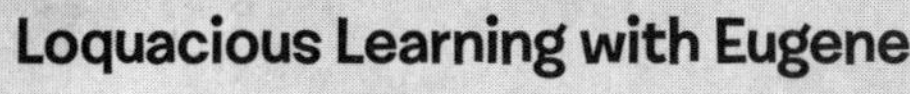

Loquacious Learning with Eugene

The biblical illustration of wineskins in verse 17 is difficult to understand since we don't commonly use them in modern times. Essentially, they were bags where people kept their wine, but they couldn't be reused. Perhaps another way of illustrating the point would be putting a new banana into an old, already-used banana peel. Or perhaps 500 gigabytes of memory into an old computer that can only accommodate 100 gigabytes. Now that would be a disaster. Suffice it to say, the Old Way couldn't contain all that the New Way offered. And I'm even more thankful for that than I am for a computer with a lot of memory.

What would you have wanted from your friend in the above scenario? Someone to sit with you, listen, maybe make you laugh a little, ask a few questions about how you're doing . . . just be there because she cared, not out of obligation. Simply put, you'd want her to act out of a heart of genuine care and interest.

Jesus longs for that kind of relationship with us. He desires for us to know Him—really know Him by spending time with Him. Not simply doing things *for* Him.

Challenge

Get a journal and start writing letters to God on a regular basis. Tell Him about your thoughts and feelings, just like a friend would talk to a friend.

Devo 30

Great Faith

Read Matthew 9:18–34.

What if someone told you that if you walked into the woods, found a possum with golden eyes, and handed it twenty bucks, you would save the world from a mutant insect invasion?

You probably wouldn't do it, because that would be pretty weird. But get a load of what God asked Noah to do . . .

In Genesis chapters 6–9 (and in the *Odyssey* episode "By Faith, Noah" (album 4), God asks Noah to build an enormous boat (or ark) because He is going to destroy the wicked world with a flood. Oh, and God tells Noah to fill the whole thing with animals. It takes Noah many years to construct the ark, but the Bible never says that he questions God's command. All it says is "Noah did everything just as God commanded him" (6:22).

God's instructions must have seemed ridiculous to Noah at the time. But Noah obeyed God anyway. And because he did, he is listed in the Bible's Faith Hall of Fame as someone who had great faith in God (Hebrews 11:7).

In today's passage, Jesus healed a bunch of people. Those people had one thing in common: They all had great faith. A temple leader told Jesus, "My daughter has just died. But come and put your hand on her, and she will live" (Matthew 9:18). And the woman who was bleeding said to herself, "If I only touch his cloak, I will be healed" (verse 20). Because of the faith of this temple leader and the sick woman, Jesus healed the woman and the temple leader's daughter.

God can do amazing things in our lives when we have faith in Him. And when we trust Him, we're more likely to obey Him. We're more likely to give our money

Connie's Corner

Have you ever heard the phrase *a leap of faith*? It means that you take a risk in the hope that God will bless you. Well, my church once had a Leap Year of Faith. It was a leap year, and we wanted to do something special. So everyone decided to do stuff like give a bigger offering or pray more or tell more people about Jesus than ever before. We did that for an entire year! And wow, did God ever do some amazing things! Our church grew, my faith got stronger, and all sorts of people came to know Jesus as their Savior. It was really great!

to the poor if we have faith He's going to provide for us. We're more likely to do what the Bible says if we have faith that the Bible is the true Word of God. We're more likely to pray when we have faith that God is listening.

Trust God and watch Him work!

Daily Challenge

Think of one person who would be reluctant to come to church with you. Then pray for that person every day. Treat that person like a special friend. After a few weeks, invite him or her to church. Have faith that God will bless your efforts, and see what happens.

Devo 31

The Harvest

Read Matthew 9:35–38.

On Wednesday, your mother says the most dreaded thing you could possibly imagine: "You have to clean your room on Saturday." You gulp. You open the door to your room. You scan it quickly. You try to remember where your bed is. Is it underneath the mountain of dirty clothes? Games, marbles, and stuffed animals still block the closet door from your sleepover weeks ago. You sniff a month-old hot dog on a stick from underneath the dresser. You decide right then that this isn't a one-person job.

You get on the phone and call in reinforcements. Your first call is to Gary the Human Forklift. He can help lift the laundry. Then you call Mary the Mad Organizer. She's the one who puts all of her homework in folders with color-coded tabs. She'll be able to organize the closet. Then you call Barry the Exterminator. He hunts with his father and can make excellent snares for animals. He can capture any rodents that happen to be living underneath the bed.

You get everyone lined up to come over to your house at nine o'clock on Saturday morning. But then the unthinkable happens. A snowstorm hits on Friday night. No one can come over. Suddenly you're left to clean your room all by yourself. You hyperventilate a little as you listen to the tiny rodents under your bed gnawing and squeaking. They seem to be mocking you . . .

In today's Bible reading, Jesus was talking about another kind of overwhelming task when He said to His disciples, "The harvest is plentiful but the workers are few" (Matthew 9:37). The word *harvest* refers to the people who need to hear about Jesus. The term *workers* refers to the evangelists and missionaries who need to tell people the good news.

Loquacious Learning with Eugene

There are roughly twenty-nine billion people in the world who have never heard the good news about Jesus.[1] That many people would fill the Indianapolis Speedway more than eleven thousand times! (The Indianapolis Speedway is the largest stadium in the world, with a seating capacity of 250,000 people.)[2] We certainly have a lot of work to do as believers! But as it says in Matthew 19:26, "With God all things are possible."

So many people in the world know nothing about Jesus, who loves them and can save them from their sins. He's the only Savior who can give them hope and new lives. But it's our job to go out and tell them about Him (more on this in the next devotion). It's hard work, and it can seem as if there is too much to do. That's why it's important to pray for more workers to tell others about Jesus.

Daily Challenge

Every day this week, pray for more workers to help tell people the good news about Jesus.

Devo 32

Rejected, but Not Dejected

Read Matthew 10:1–16.

In the *Odyssey* episode "Go Ye Therefore" (album 4), Connie decides to spread the good news about Jesus, and nothing will stop her. She is determined to tell as many people about the Savior as she can.

It turns out to be a lot harder than she thinks. She tries to hand out Christian pamphlets in the park, but most people ignore her. One person tears up the pamphlet right in front of her face. Then she tries to put the pamphlets in books at the bookstore, but the owner throws her out. Then she covers her mother's car with Christian bumper stickers. But when her mother comes home, she thinks her car has been vandalized. All of Connie's attempts fail miserably until her friend Cheryl tells her that she has been watching Connie and has noticed a big difference in Connie's life. Cheryl wants to know more about what has changed Connie so much. Connie is happy to tell Cheryl about Jesus.

Jesus told His disciples that they weren't going to win everyone over with the good news. Some people won't listen when you want to talk about God with them. But don't worry. Keep praying for them and wait for the right opportunity. In the meantime, share the good news with people who show an interest in learning about Jesus.

When you try to share the good news with others, you'll probably face rejection, too. People who aren't open to hearing about Jesus may make fun of you. And far more people will say no than yes. But that's okay. Sometime soon one person will listen. Don't give up!

There's an old story about a girl on a beach. The tide came in high and then receded, leaving hundreds of starfish on the beach. If the starfish didn't get back

Wandering with Wooton

As a mailman, I know a thing or two about rejection. People always get mad when they get nothing but junk mail. One time a guy threw a handful of baked goods at me for bringing him a catalog for Luxurious Locks Hair Care Salon. He was bald. Sometimes the same thing happens when I tell people about Jesus. Many people don't want to hear about His love, and that can hurt. But it doesn't stop me from trying. The message of Jesus is too important to keep to myself.

into the ocean, they would die. So the girl began to walk down the beach, throwing starfish into the ocean one at a time. A man walked up and noticed her efforts. He glanced down the beach and saw hundreds of starfish still stranded. He said, "Why are you doing this? You'll never get them all; there are too many. What you're doing doesn't matter."

The girl held up a starfish and responded, "It matters to this one." And she tossed it back into the ocean.[1]

You're never going to reach everyone with the message of Jesus. Share it anyway.

Daily Challenge

Think of someone who isn't a Christian. Tell that person the starfish story and then let that person know he or she is special to God.

Devo 33

Speaking Through You

Read Matthew 10:17–20.

Often, churchgoers are given bulletins or programs when they come through the door. This tells them which songs are going to be sung, which Bible verses will be read, and what the title of the preacher's sermon is.

The Quakers have none of that. Traditional Quakers are a religious group that has almost no structure to their worship services. They walk into the church building in silence, and for a while no one speaks or even moves. Then someone who feels as if God is speaking to him or her stands up. That person speaks and then sits down. Everyone sits in silence again. Then someone else stands up and tells the crowd what he or she feels as if God is saying. This goes on and on.

Four hundred years ago, these types of services would last for hours. No preacher. No songs. No morning announcements to tell people about the potluck dinner after church. Just people speaking when they felt led to speak.[1]

The Quakers must really like what Jesus said in today's Bible passage. He told His disciples not to worry about what to say when they were arrested and had to testify about Him in court (Matthew 10:19). They didn't have to figure out what to say on their own. The Holy Spirit would speak through them.

When it comes to telling others about Jesus, you don't have to worry about writing anything down or practicing what to say. God will give you the words.

That's a really comforting thing to know, isn't it? It can be nerve-racking to share the gospel, because you never know how people are going to respond. But this is one of the great things about becoming a Christian. When you ask Jesus to come into your life, God gives you the gift of the Holy Spirit. The Holy Spirit is

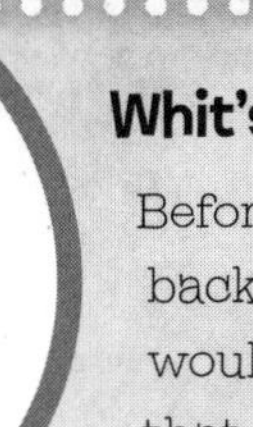

Whit's Wisdom

Before Jesus left the disciples and went back up to heaven, He told them that He would never actually leave them. He said that the Holy Spirit would be there with them all the time. Not only that, but the Holy Spirit would give them the power to reach people all over the world. The disciples must have been surprised to hear about Jesus' ambitious plans for them. But Jesus was right. People all around the world have heard the good news through missionaries, preachers, and people like you.

always right there with you. He gives you the courage and the right words to say when you want to tell someone about Jesus. This is one of the best gifts because it's easy to get tongue-tied in these kinds of situations.

Don't hesitate to tell others about how great Jesus is. The Holy Spirit will be there to help you.

Daily Challenge

Think of one person who needs to know what you know about Jesus. Begin thinking of ways to approach him or her, and pray that God will give you the right words to say about Jesus.

Devo 34

The Door

Read Matthew 10:21–36.

You're walking along and suddenly come to a fork in the road. Pointing down the left path is a sign that says, "One Mile Ahead—Mockery, Rejection, Pain, Punishment, Time in Prison." Pointing down the right path is a sign that says "One Mile Ahead—Rest, Relaxation, Fun, Ignorant Bliss." Which path would you take?

Most people would follow the path on the right. It's easier.

The apostle Paul didn't know everything that would happen to him when he chose to follow Christ. Not only did he endure great pain, but he also said that we should "rejoice in our sufferings, because . . . suffering produces perseverance" (Romans 5:3).

While social persecution happens to every Christian at some point, it's unlikely that believers in the United States will face the kind of physical persecution the apostle Paul suffered. In Paul's day, beatings for lawbreakers were common, and that fact alone shows just how seriously he took his duty to preach the gospel to others.

In Matthew 10, Jesus warned His disciples to expect problems as His followers. He said that telling people the good news would be hard. The disciples would have to leave their homes behind and travel light. They would even face rejection, persecution, and death. Some of the disciples struggled along the way. They ran away, hid, and denied that they even knew Jesus. But ultimately, they faced persecution for Jesus' sake and had the courage to die while proclaiming the good news that He came to save us all.

Loquacious Learning with Eugene

Merriam-Webster's Collegiate Dictionary defines a *martyr* as "a person who voluntarily suffers death as the penalty of witnessing to and refusing to renounce a religion." The first Christian martyr was Stephen, who was stoned to death for preaching about Jesus. Though it might be tempting to think only of the tragedy of that event, it's important to remember that Stephen's death also set in motion a wave of activity that led to millions of new Christian churches being started around the world.

It makes the normal excuses for not sharing the gospel seem kind of silly, doesn't it? What keeps us from telling our friends about Jesus or simply asking them to come to church with us? Fear of embarrassment? Fear of rejection? Fear of getting tongue-tied?

There's a fork in the road ahead. Which path will you take?

Daily Challenge

With your parents' permission, use the Internet or books to do some research about the life of a Christian martyr (someone who died for his or her faith). Examples are Joan of Arc, Dietrich Bonhoeffer, or Jim Elliot. Pray for boldness to speak out about Jesus as they did.

Devo 35

The Last Cookie

Read Matthew 10:37–42.

A huge crowd is gathered outside city hall. There is a collective gasp as the cover is lifted off the new statue that will sit in front of the building for all eternity. The statue is made of beautiful bronze, and a plaque on the bottom reads "Joey Meyers—the boy who gave the last cookie to his brother." The crowd erupts in wild applause as Joey steps to the podium. He says, "The day I gave the last cookie to my little brother started like any other day . . ."

Joey tells the crowd that there was only one cookie left in the jar. He wrestled with what he should do with the cookie. *Should I eat it? Should I leave it for my brother? I already had three cookies today. My brother will like it if I leave the last one for him.* Joey decided to let his brother have the cookie.

After finishing his story, Joey steps down from the stage. There isn't a dry eye in the place.

In real life, no statues are sculpted for people who leave the last cookie for their brothers. But perhaps there should be. Making significant sacrifices for others is hard.

The challenge in today's Bible reading is even harder. Jesus talked to His disciples about the rejection they'd face. He talked about persecution, and then He described the sacrifices His disciples would have to make. The crazy thing is that it's one of the first conversations Jesus had with all twelve of His disciples after He called them to follow Him.

Jesus didn't start with all the great things about following Him. He didn't say, "If you follow Me, you'll get ten vacation days, unlimited coffee, and a company

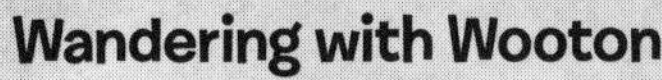

Wandering with Wooton

Once after I heard a sermon about sacrifice, I decided to sacrifice the money I'd normally spend on licorice and give it to the church instead. I did it for a month, and boy, was it hard! I didn't know how many things would remind me of red licorice whips—like my neighbor's daughter's jump rope (she cried when I almost ate it). And my garden hose. And black licorice whips! But I made it, and my church donated the money to a food pantry. All that sacrifice was worth it!

donkey!" No, He started with the tough stuff. It's a wonder that the disciples didn't just pack up and leave right then and there.

Jesus knew that following Him would be a sacrifice for them. And it is for us too. It's a sacrifice to think of others before yourself. It's hard to put God first. You might sacrifice a TV show so that you have time to read your Bible. You might even give your hard-earned money to the church or to the poor. But Jesus also knew that the sacrifices His disciples made would be worth it!

Sacrificing is more than just your gift to God. It's God's gift to you. He blesses those who put themselves second.

Daily Challenge

Give up something for a week, like television, video games, comic books, or candy. Use the time or money you save in a way that will glorify God.

Follow the Rules?

The Pharisees paid more attention to what all their rules were than to why they followed them in the first place. Follow the maze from the arrow to the period to discover what God considers more important than any rules. Check out Galatians 5:6 if you need a hint.

Puzzle #5

___ _____ ______ _____

________ ___ ______

_____________ ________

_________ ____.

Answer on page 209.

Devo 36

No Doubt

Read Matthew 11:1–24.

"If it looks like a duck, swims like a duck, and quacks like a duck, then it probably is a duck." Have you ever heard this statement? It's another way of saying that if all the evidence points to something being true, it's probably true. For instance, if you're coughing, sneezing, and stuffed up, and on top of that, you have a fever, your stomach feels like it's flipped inside-out, and your brain is tricking you into thinking that there's a talking bear wearing a birthday hat in your room, then you're probably sick.

In today's Bible passage, Jesus gave John the Baptist some valuable advice for dealing with doubt.

Hundreds of years before John was born, the prophet Malachi talked about him: "I will send my messenger, who will prepare the way before me" (Malachi 3:1). John's job was to tell people that a Savior was on His way. John talked about repentance and the kingdom of heaven before Jesus actually appeared on the scene (Matthew 3:1–3). When John began preaching to the Jewish people, he very likely wondered about the coming Savior. Was He already born? What would He look like? Would John recognize Him when He arrived?

John was in prison by the time he heard about the wonderful things Jesus was doing—healing people, preaching, performing miracles—and he wanted to know if this was truly the Savior he'd been preaching about for so long. So he sent word to ask Jesus that very question.

Jesus told John's disciples to go back and tell John to look at the evidence: "The blind receive sight, the lame walk, those who have leprosy are cured, the deaf hear, the dead are raised, and the good news is preached to the poor" (Matthew

Connie's Corner

People like Eugene call me stubborn, but I'm not, and nothing will ever get me to admit it! Ever! Okay, maybe I'm a little stubborn, but I know where I get it from—my mom. For many years she didn't believe in Jesus even though she saw how much of a difference He had made in my life. Finally she saw enough of the evidence to realize that Jesus was real and that she needed Him to be her Savior, too. It was a great day!

11:5). John probably thought, *With all of that evidence, Jesus must be the Savior I've been telling everyone about.*

If you ever doubt whether there is a God who loves you, just look at the evidence. The stars, the mountains, the oceans, the human body, lightning, music, and even the long-tailed brush lizard are all evidence of a Creator who cares enough about us to give us a beautiful world to live in and enjoy.

Daily Challenge

With your parents' permission, use the Internet or books to do some research on the human body, outer space, or the ocean. (If you're doing your research online, type "amazing facts about _____" or "surprising facts about _____" into your search engine and then add the topic. For example: "amazing facts about platypuses." See the evidence of a great God as you discover how amazing His creations are.

Devo 37

Come to Me

Read Matthew 11:25–30.

The 1950s was a difficult time in the United States. World War II was still fresh in the memories of most Americans. It was a time when the nation needed some rest from the terrible stress of war. But then another war sprung up in Asia in 1950. The Korean War spoiled peacetime. Countries around the world were building nuclear bombs. Newspapers, television, and books were constantly reminding people that if those bombs were used, it could mean World War III. It's the kind of stuff that might put you on edge, huh?

The Korean War ended in 1953, but everyone was worried about the possibility of a nuclear war. A few years later, in 1958, a fourteen-year-old boy from England named Laurie London brought back a song that slaves once sang. It was called "He's Got the Whole World in His Hands." The simple lyrics spoke about how God has everything under control in this world. Even though it was a song you might hear in a children's Sunday school class, it became popular on the radio and climbed to the top of America's record charts.[1]

The song was so popular because the country desperately needed to hear the message that the God of peace still had everything under control. They needed to know that God could give them rest in the middle of stress and ease their troubles and worries.

What troubles do you have? Do you have a history test coming up, and you can't remember any of the Constitution beyond "We the People . . ."? Are you having trouble getting along with your friends? Does it always seem as if your parents are mad at you? Whatever your difficulties may be, you can always go to Jesus in prayer. And remember . . .

Whit's Wisdom

It's important to remember that Jesus didn't say He would get rid of our burdens completely. He simply said He would make our burdens lighter if we gave them to Him. Our lives as Christians will have their share of problems. It's all a matter of choosing whether to deal with difficulties ourselves or allow God to help us through them. The second choice is much better.

He's got the wind and the rain in His hands
He's got the tiny little baby in His hands
He's got you and me, brother, in His hands
He's got the whole world in His hands.[2]

Daily Challenge

When you pray tonight, let God know about anything that's weighing heavy on your heart. Be honest and ask God to help you.

Devo 38

Missing the Point

Read Matthew 12:1–8.

As a way of worshipping their god, parents at a temple in India hand their one-year-old babies to clerics. The clerics take the babies to the top of the temple and toss them off. The babies drop to some men at the bottom waiting to catch them with a sheet. Worshippers believe this ceremony appeases their god so he'll grant their children health, intelligence, bravery, and luck.[1]

You may be wondering why they didn't just feed their children spinach and put them in soccer camp to make them healthy.

As silly as this form of worship sounds, the Pharisees in Jesus' day had some weird ideas about worship too. As we learned in devo 8, the Pharisees wigged out about the laws on the Sabbath (the day of worship). You could do no work on the Sabbath. None. You weren't even allowed to carry things. If you swatted at a fly on the Sabbath, that was considered hunting. It was forbidden.

In today's Bible passage, the Pharisees complained that Jesus' disciples were picking grain on the Sabbath. He reminded them that He was "Lord of the Sabbath" (Matthew 12:8). They had been putting so much emphasis on worship that they had forgotten the God they were supposed to be worshipping.

In the *Odyssey* episode "Sunday Morning Scramble" (album 43), the Washingtons rush to get to church on Sunday morning and forget the reason they are going in the first place. Tom Riley calms them down and asks if they would like to join him in prayer to prepare for worship. The Washingtons realize, *Oh yeah. Worshipping God. That's what we're supposed to be doing!*

God doesn't care about religious rituals, like throwing babies off high temple

Connie's Corner

My favorite psalm is Psalm 100. It talks a lot about worship—about shouting for joy, coming before God with songs, giving thanks to Him, and entering His courts with praise. It sounds like those things were missing from the Pharisees' worship of God. Joy. Thankfulness. Praise. When we worship God, He commands us to be joyful, offer thanksgiving, and give Him praise. Church always makes me appreciate how good God is. I think that's kind of the point.

towers. He cares that we worship Him in our hearts. It's easy to forget a very simple concept: The God whom we worship is more important than the way we worship.

Daily Challenge

Try something different tonight when you have your prayer time with God. Start by singing a song of praise to Him. Or making a list of all the things you're thankful for. Take some time and think about your awesome God.

Devo 39

Missing the Point Again

Read Matthew 12:9–14.

Jenny, Jerry, and Jessie burst out the front door. Jenny hopped on one foot to put on her second shoe as she ran down the front sidewalk after her friends.

Jessie looked back. "Come on, Jenny!" They raced down the street like cheetahs after their prey.

As they passed the park, they saw a little girl sitting on a park bench crying. But there was no time to find out why. They ran on. As they passed the houses on Third Street, they noticed an old man struggling to carry a heavy garbage bag down his driveway.

He shouldn't have filled up the bag so much, thought Jerry as the trio scurried past.

As they ran by the post office, a woman called out to them. Her arm was stuck in the mailbox, and she couldn't get it out.

Oh, well, thought Jessie, *there's a mail collection at this box at three o'clock. The mail carrier will help her then.*

Just then, Jenny stopped for a moment to catch her breath. Jessie turned around, annoyed. "Hurry up, Jenny! We're gonna be late for Bible study!"

Jenny, Jerry, and Jessie kind of missed the point, didn't they? The Pharisees weren't much better. Once again they harped on Jesus because He broke their rules. In today's Bible passage, Jesus healed a man with a shriveled hand on the Sabbath. Jesus did not put the Jewish religious traditions before helping others.

There are other more important rules that the Pharisees forgot about. Like the rule God gave us to love our neighbors. Or the rule Jesus gave us to put others before ourselves.

Wandering with Wooton

One time I went on a diet, and I bought a book about what I should and shouldn't be eating. When I read the list of things I shouldn't be eating, it made me so hungry that I went out and bought pretty much everything on the list! It was a bad week, and I shouldn't have given in. I guess that's kind of like reading the Bible every day and then doing the complete opposite of what it says. A great verse is James 1:22: "Do not merely listen to the word. . . . Do what it says."

Sometimes we get wrapped up in the small stuff and forget about the really important things. Going to a Bible study is a good thing. God wants us to learn as much as we can about His Word. But what's the point of going to a Bible study if we don't do what the Bible says we should do?

Daily Challenge

Pray for opportunities to help people, and then look for ways to do it. See if your neighbors, friends, or siblings have any needs, and do what you can to meet those needs.

Devo 40

Filling the Stadium

Read Matthew 12:15–21.

The Beatles, a very popular musical group in the 1960s, sang a song that went like this:

> We all live in a yellow submarine
> Yellow submarine, yellow submarine[1]

Deep lyrics, huh? Poetry like this makes you want to go out and change the world, doesn't it? In the 1960s, the Beatles played concerts for sold-out crowds all around the world. Since that time, they've sold more than two billion albums![2] So many people are dying to hear about a brightly colored underwater craft that doubles as an apartment complex.

Sometimes we idolize strange people, don't we? Musicians, athletes, and actors are often followed by people who take pictures of them and wait with bated breath to hear any word that comes out of their mouths. And what words come out of their mouths? A lot of times it's nonsense.

At least some people in Jesus' time had it right. Today's Bible passage tells us that crowds followed Jesus around a lot. In fact, He often had to take some time off to get away from them. Why did they love Jesus so much? Because He preached the truth. He had messages of victory and justice and hope to offer them. They wanted to hear about God from someone who knew Him intimately. Is there anyone better to learn from than God's only Son?

It's easy for us to get caught up in following the popular people of our day.

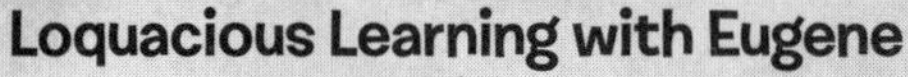

Loquacious Learning with Eugene

Recently a writer for an influential website listed the ten living people he would most like to meet. His list included four singers, three athletes, two actors, and a puppet. When I compiled my own list, it was a bit dissimilar. It included two scientists, three mathematicians, three anthropologists, and . . . well, the aforementioned puppet. It's truly a fascinating puppet. This article was an interesting study of the types of people we admire. But at the top of my list was the living person I would most like to meet: Jesus Christ.

But sometimes we have to remember who speaks the truth and who speaks about things that are worthless. A good question to ask yourself is "If Jesus came back and walked the earth today, would you be in the crowd following Him, or would you be in the crowd following the teenage boy band that makes young girls faint and scream?"

Live with Jesus. Not in a yellow submarine.

Daily Challenge

Make a list of people you spend the most time with. Are they people who help others? Are they people who have wisdom? Are they people who can teach you good things?

Devo 41

Pick a Side

Read Matthew 12:22–37.

Red Rover is a confusing game, isn't it? Two teams line up across from each other, and the members of each team hold hands. One team then calls on a member of the other team to break through the line. They say, "Red Rover, Red Rover, let Marcy come over!" Marcy then tries to forcefully break through the interlocked hands of two people. (This game is also responsible for many emergency room visits!) If Marcy is unable to break through the hands, she has to switch teams. Suddenly all of Marcy's loyalties change.

It's really hard to have any team pride in Red Rover. One minute you're on one team, and the next you're on the other. Those signs you made the night before the big Red Rover match are worthless—the ones that say "Go Lions!" Because three minutes into the game, you're no longer a Lion; you're a Bear.

In today's Bible passage, the Pharisees didn't seem to understand which team they were on. After Jesus drove a demon out of a man, they accused Him of using some kind of devil magic. Jesus told them they weren't making any sense. He said that if He were on the devil's team, why would He throw out the demons?

Jesus got fed up with the Pharisees and basically told them, "Pick a side! This is a war between good and evil. Why are you fighting against me?" The Pharisees were causing more harm than good by forgetting who the real enemy is—the devil.

The devil is real, and he wants you to come over to his side. You know that little voice in your head that tells you to do something you know is wrong? That's the devil trying to tempt you. It's very easy to listen to that voice and go over to his side, just like an unsuccessful Red Rover opponent.

Whit's Wisdom

Time and time again in the book of Matthew, Jesus argued with the Pharisees. He argued with them more than anyone else. Why? Because the Pharisees acted as if they were on God's side, when, in fact, they were drawing others away from God. Those are the most dangerous kinds of people. We should always look out for those who pretend to be Christians but are actually teaching us things that Jesus never would have said.

But Jesus tells us how to keep from switching sides. He called it "bearing fruit." This means that we do the things that make us Christians. We trust Jesus and let Him have control of our lives. We pray. We read the Bible. We obey the things we're taught. If we stay focused on Jesus, we won't focus so much on the things that are tempting us.

Bear good fruit and stay on the winning team.

Daily Challenge

Think of a sin you struggle with daily. Is it disobeying your parents? Wasting time? Using words you shouldn't? Fighting with your brother or sister? Pray that God will give you the strength to say no to the devil, and choose to bear good fruit the next time you are faced with that temptation.

Devo 42

The Stubborn Hall of Fame

Read Matthew 12:38–45.

Who do you think should be in the Stubborn Hall of Fame? This organization celebrates the famously pigheaded. One good choice would be the pharaoh in Exodus 5–15 of the Bible. Pharaoh was the leader of Egypt and had many false gods. Egypt had many slaves called the Israelites. God wanted to set the Israelites free, and He sent Moses to demand that Pharaoh let His people go. But Pharaoh wouldn't do it. So God gave Pharaoh a little demonstration of His power and turned the nearby Nile River into blood. When Moses went back to Pharaoh, Pharaoh wouldn't budge. He refused to set the slaves free. So God sent another plague—this time frogs came out of nowhere and filled the land. Slimy, noisy frogs were everywhere!

Still, Pharaoh stubbornly refused to let God's people go. So God sent seven more plagues, including gnats, flies, disease, hail, locusts, and darkness. But Pharaoh said no again and again. He wouldn't just admit that God was in control. It took one final plague—the deaths of Pharaoh's son and army—to make Pharaoh realize that the God of the Israelites was more powerful than any man or any Egyptian false god out there.

The Pharisees could also have been in the Stubborn Hall of Fame. In today's Bible passage, they asked Jesus if He could perform a miracle for them. Maybe a quick lightning bolt or something? But Jesus refused because He knew the Pharisees wouldn't believe that He was God even if Jesus did produce a lightning bolt. Jesus said that years ago people came from miles around to hear the wisdom of King Solomon. The stuff Jesus talked about was far wiser than anything Solomon came up with, and the Pharisees wouldn't even cross the street to listen.

Wandering with Wooton

Have you ever heard the phrase *stubborn as a mule*? Well, the only mule I ever knew personally was named Ralph. He belonged to my great uncle and was actually very obedient, helping at the farm all day. So I don't really get that phrase. Maybe another phrase would work better, like "stubborn as Wooton when he doesn't want to go to the dentist, even when it feels like he has a porcupine in his mouth." We can all be pretty hardheaded. It would be much better if we were all a little more like Ralph. Ralph also ate a lot of apples. Woo-hoo! Fiber!

The fact is, they didn't believe in Jesus because they didn't *want* to believe Him. Does that sound familiar? Sometimes we can be stubborn too. We don't want to admit that God and our parents are right. News flash: Both God and your parents are smarter than you. Do what they say. You don't want your picture next to the Pharisees in the Stubborn Hall of Fame.

Daily Challenge

What are some things you're stubborn about? Homework? Eating vegetables? Doing chores? Letting friends or siblings take their turns first? This week, stay out of the Stubborn Hall of Fame and cheerfully do the very things you hate doing.

Signs of the Savior

When John the Baptist's followers asked Jesus if He was "the one who was to come," Jesus gave a great answer. To find out what the answer is, use the key below to decode Matthew 11:5.

	1	2	3	4	5	6
A	W	Y	T	M	D	H
B	V	S	L	C	G	P
C	R	K	B	F	O	U
D	I	A	E	N		

___ ___ ___   ___ ___ ___ ___ ___
A3 A6 D3   C3 B3 D1 D4 A5

___ ___ ___ ___ ___ ___ ___   ___ ___ ___ ___ ___
C1 D3 B4 D3 D1 B1 D3   B2 D1 B5 A6 A3,

___ ___ ___   ___ ___ ___ ___   ___ ___ ___ ___
A3 A6 D3   B3 D2 A4 D3   A1 D2 B3 C2,

___ ___ ___ ___ ___   ___ ___ ___   ___ ___ ___ ___
A3 A6 C5 B2 D3   A1 A6 C5   A6 D2 B1 D3

B3 D3 B6 C1 C5 B2 A2   D2 C1 D3

B4 C6 C1 D3 A5,   A3 A6 D3

A5 D3 D2 C4   A6 D3 D2 C1,   A3 A6 D3

A5 D3 D2 A5   D2 C1 D3

C1 D2 D1 B2 D3 A5,   D2 D4 A5   A3 A6 D3

B5 C5 C5 A5   D4 D3 A1 B2   D1 B2

B6 C1 D3 D2 B4 A6 D3 A5   A3 C5

A3 A6 D3   B6 C5 C5 C1.

Answer on page 209.

Devo 43

The Family of God

Read Matthew 12:46–50.

Marlah was an orphan living in Malawi, Africa. Her parents died when she was seven. At ten, she was on her own. Every day she had to find her own food if she wanted to eat, and there wasn't much around. In Malawi, even the ants starve. She had no bed, only some hay in between two houses that she lay down on. When she played with friends during the day, their mothers would call to them when they wanted them home for the night. Marlah had no one calling her home. She hadn't had a hug in three years.

Then one day, a family from America came to her village. They met Marlah and found out she was an orphan. They told Marlah that she was going to come to America to live with them. Marlah didn't understand at first, but in a few months, it happened. Marlah flew on her very first airplane to the state of Ohio. She couldn't believe the size of the buildings she saw. Her new adoptive parents took her to her first restaurant, where she was served as much food as she could possibly eat. When she got to her new home, she played with electronic toys and slept on a mattress, both for the first time. At bedtime her new parents prayed with her and then gave her a hug and a kiss before she fell asleep.

On Marlah's first day of school, the kids all asked her, "What's your favorite thing about America? The food? The houses? The toys? Riding around in nice cars?"

Marlah shook her head and replied, "The hugs."

For the first time in years, Marlah belonged to a family.

Being part of a loving family is a very special thing. It means we're not alone.

Connie's Corner

When my parents got divorced, it was probably the worst day of my life. My family was torn apart. But then I moved to Odyssey, where I met Whit. And after a while, I became a Christian. In a way I felt like my family was restored a little bit because I was becoming a member of a new family–the family of God. This family can never be broken up. That was the best day of my life!

It means we have people who take care of us because they love us. A loving family is made up of people who want to be around to watch us grow up.

When we become Christians, Jesus makes us part of His family. We're just as important to Him as His actual mother or brothers. He loves us and wants to be around to watch us grow up.

Daily Challenge

Make something special for Jesus, just as you'd make something special for your mother or father. Make Him a card, write Him a poem, or color Him a picture. Thank Him for making you part of His family.

Devo 44

The Sower and the Seeds

Read Matthew 13:1–23.

Jesus often used parables to teach His disciples about the kingdom of God. Parables are short stories that teach some truth or moral. In today's Bible passage, Jesus told His disciples the parable of the sower. In the *Odyssey* episode "Scattered Seeds" (album 7), the gang at Whit's End played out this parable on stage in a Little Theater play that Connie directed called *Scattered Seeds.*

The kids lived out the parable behind the scenes as well. Jesus' parable used seeds to symbolize people who experience the words of God in different ways. Eugene became the seed that was snatched up by the birds when his college computer club snatched him from the play. Monty was like the seed that fell among the rocks. He was very excited about the play at first, but then he lost interest when things became hard. Jenny, a perfectionist, worried that people wouldn't like her if she didn't do a perfect job on the play. She choked, just like the seed that fell among the thorns. Lucy and Tom became the seeds that were planted in good soil and produced a bumper crop. They stuck with the play, worked hard, and produced a show that everyone enjoyed.

What does the parable of the sower teach us? First, don't be afraid to ask questions. The Bible can be a tough book to figure out at times. So ask someone you trust when you don't understand what you read in the Bible.

Second, the Bible can get you excited, but don't rely on feelings all the time. You should read and study the Bible even when you don't feel like it. It isn't always easy to follow Jesus. In fact, sometimes it can be really hard. But don't get discouraged. Pray and keep on following Him!

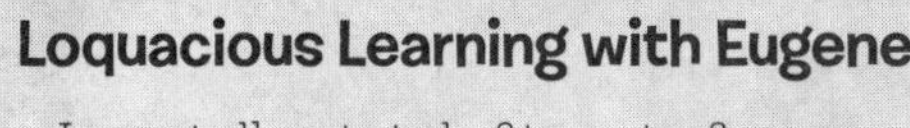

Loquacious Learning with Eugene

Jesus tells a total of twenty-four parables in the book of Matthew alone,[1] so it was clearly a favorite teaching device for Him. The concept of a parable dates back to ancient storytellers, the most famous of whom is Aesop. Fables and parables differ in that fables generally involve animals, while parables have human characters. There's a reason these tales have lasted so long. Everyone loves a story! And there is much to learn from them, especially from the parables Jesus told.

The third lesson Jesus' parable teaches us is to get rid of distractions. The devil wants to keep us from growing in our knowledge of Jesus and in our faith. So he puts all sorts of things in our lives to distract us from what's really important. Think about the way you spend your time and ask God to help you put Him first. Spend less time watching television and playing video games. Guard against bad influences, and consider your outside activities. Do you really need to be in three sports or multiple dance classes? Can you cut back on those commitments so that you have more time to study the Bible?

Fourth, the parable of the sower teaches us to study the Word of God. Believe it, love it, and make it a part of your life. Do this, and you'll produce great things for God.

Daily Challenge

Underline anything you come across in the Bible that you don't understand. Then find an adult—your parents, a family friend, your Sunday school teacher, or a pastor—and ask that person about it. Never get tired of learning about God!

Devo 45

One Fish, Two Fish, Good Fish, Bad Fish

Read Matthew 13:24–30; 36–43; 47–52.

Aaron, a boy in the fourth grade, met a crazy scientist who invented a pair of glasses that could show whether a person was evil. Anytime Aaron put on the glasses, evil people showed up green. He had fun with the glasses at first because he liked being able to distinguish evil people from good people. But then one day he put on his glasses, and his own grandmother turned green! He couldn't believe that Granny was up to something bad. Was she an enemy spy for the government? Did her walker turn into a deadly weapon? Did her false teeth become fangs in the middle of the night?

Aaron came to realize that the glasses were wrong. His grandmother was actually a sweet, gentle, kind, loving, soft-spoken woman . . . who happened to be able to shoot lasers out of her eyes!

Wouldn't this make a great movie? All right, maybe it wouldn't be such a great movie. But wouldn't it be nice if you had something like those glasses to show you whether a person is trustworthy? Or point out evil in the world? It's really hard to tell what's evil and what's good, isn't it? The parables Jesus told in today's Bible passage point out that evil hides very well—weeds in the middle of the wheat and bad fish in the middle of good ones.

Have you ever heard the phrase "Nice guys finish last"? Sometimes it feels that way, doesn't it? Bad people seem to get all the breaks. It seems as if they have more money than we do. Or they're more popular and have more fun.

But the truth is, evildoers don't actually have more fun. The fun doesn't last, and it usually ends in regret and pain. Jesus tells us in these parables that one day

Whit's Wisdom

The weeds Jesus talked about in this parable were probably a kind of grass called *darnel*. Unlike garden weeds, it was very hard to tell darnel from wheat.[1] In fact, it was a common practice for people to throw darnel seeds into the wheat fields of their enemies because it would hurt the crops. Evil thrown into the middle of good is always destructive.

evil will lose and good will win. Those weeds in the wheat field will be pulled out and thrown into fire. And the bad fish will be separated from the good fish. It may take a long time for this to happen, but be patient. Good will win out, nice guys who put their faith in Christ will finish first, and Jesus will sit on His throne as the King of our world. So don't let the weeds and rotten fish in this world discourage you.

Daily Challenge

Think about a movie or true story in which it seemed as if evil people won. Tell the story to a friend or parent, and tell them you're glad that one day, stories like this will never happen.

Devo 46

No Small Thing

Read Matthew 13:31–35.

We all know that small things can have a big impact. A microchip the size of a fingernail can contain as much information as an entire library. The Black Death, a disease that spread in Europe in the 1300s, killed more than two hundred million people.[1] It was caused by a flea the size of a pinhead.[2] The actor Tom Cruise is only five feet, seven inches tall, but his movies have made more than eight billion dollars![3]

But none of this compares to the impact of one little Baby. Jesus came to a very lost world and ended up saving it.

In today's Bible passage, Jesus compared the kingdom of God to a mustard seed. This is one of the smallest seeds that exists, and yet the bush that comes from it can grow up to ten feet tall. Jesus knew from the very beginning that the Christian church was going to get big. And not just mustard-tree big. REALLY BIG!

The book of Acts tells us that after Jesus rose from the dead and went back to heaven, the apostle Peter and the Christian church spread the news about Him to the ends of the earth. Today there are more than two billion Christians in the world—a third of the entire world population![4] A God who can make something grow that big deserves our attention, don't you think? If God is that powerful, don't you think He can help you with the problems you face? Like helping you get along better with your sister? Or helping you on your math test? God is bigger than your problems. We're going to hear more about the mustard seed later, and about how much faith it takes to change the world. But for now remember that God can take even your smallest efforts and do big things with them.

Wandering with Wooton

Once I tried to take a picture of a mustard seed with the Grand Canyon in Arizona in the background. I thought it would be really artistic, you know? I thought it would show how you can see God in the smallest things and in the biggest things. But I ended up dropping the seed, and it fell about five hundred feet down into the canyon. So I went home. But the Grand Canyon was cool. You should go.

Daily Challenge

With your parents' permission, do some research about missionaries who have seen the impact of Jesus on people around the world. Look up people like William Carey, Lottie Moon, George Mueller, or Amy Carmichael. Write a journal entry about one reason you admire these missionaries.

Devo 47

The Really Expensive Pearl

Read Matthew 13:44–46.

A number of Internet surveys asked the question, "If your house was on fire, and you only had sixty seconds to get out, what would be the first things that you would grab?" The responses almost always went something like this:

Family members

Pets

Family photo albums

After those three items, the lists would vary from "laptop computer" to "car keys" to "telephone," and other items. People decided that their most prized possessions were people, then animals, then photos of people (and possibly photos of their animals). This seems like a good list because everything else can pretty much be replaced. In a moment of crisis, people have to make quick decisions about what they value the most.

In today's Bible passage, the man decided that the pearl he discovered was worth more than everything else he owned. So he sold everything he owned to buy it. Was this guy crazy? Was there a million-dollar coin inside this pearl? It might come as a surprise, but Jesus wasn't talking about the value of pearls when He told the disciples this parable. He was talking about the value of God's kingdom—the value of being a Christian. This "pearl" has more value than anything on earth, because God's kingdom lasts forever. Laptops don't.

Do you believe that having Jesus is more important than anything else in your life? When you truly believe this, it changes the way you act and think about lots of things. You begin to think differently about money and how you use your time.

Connie's Corner

Last year I kept all my receipts and figured out how much money I spent on things for the whole year. It was shocking when I found out that I spent almost twice as much on clothes, fashion magazines, and makeup as I did on tithing to my church! Half of those clothes I wore only once. I decided right then and there to change what I value. I haven't gotten the balance perfect just yet, but I'm getting better at valuing what's important.

You begin to understand what has value in God's eyes, and you want to share Jesus with people who don't know Him yet.

When you get to heaven someday, you might shake your head and wonder, *Why did I value my toys so much? Why did I watch so much television? Why didn't I care more about my neighbors?*

Stuff won't matter in heaven. So focus now on what really matters in the long run. Not even the most dazzling pearl on earth can compare to Jesus!

Daily Challenge

Make a list of the things you spend the most time doing in a day. What does this show you about what you value most? What changes can you make to put God's kingdom first?

Devo 48

The Challenge

Read Matthew 13:53–58.

K. K. Devaraj had a bright future ahead of him. In the 1980s he lived in Lebanon, where his family had made a fortune in the oil business. K. K. was a young executive in the company, and he was probably planning to live a very rich life in Lebanon.

Then someone taught him about the Bible, and he learned about Jesus. K. K. realized that, even though he could buy just about anything he wanted, his life was empty. So he became a Christian. He probably had no idea how much his life was about to change.

His family didn't share his Christian beliefs, and they disowned him. They kicked him out of the house and took away his job. If he didn't stop following Jesus, all of his money, power, and comforts would be taken away. But K. K. didn't turn his back on his faith in Christ. Instead, he turned his back on all his wealth and power. He traveled with his wife and son to Mumbai, India, and began to help everyone he could find who was hungry, poor, sick, or alone—all in the name of Jesus.

Today, K. K. is the leader of Bombay Teen Challenge, which provides shelter, food, medical care, and love to thousands of Indian children and teens. Many of the children call K. K. "Uncle" because he is the only good father figure they have ever known.

K. K. had to sacrifice a lot to do God's work. He had to turn his back on luxury, comfort, and his own family in order to follow the plans Jesus had for his life.[1]

Of course, this is nothing new. In today's Bible passage, we see that Jesus Himself was rejected by His own people. His neighbors weren't proud of Him at

Whit's Wisdom

The Bible is full of people who made great sacrifices to follow God. Noah sacrificed his time and reputation to build the ark. Matthew the tax collector gave up riches to follow Jesus. The apostle Paul gave up religious power to become a Christian. And as we'll find out tomorrow, John the Baptist lost his head! In every case, God honored the sacrifices and gave these men the ability to do amazing things.

all. Instead, they "took offense at him" (Matthew 13:57). But that didn't stop Jesus from preaching, healing, and doing exactly what God wanted Him to do.

Chances are you won't have to turn your back on your family to follow Jesus, but this is another one of those "What do you value?" questions. Are you willing to give up the things you value to do what God asks you to do? K. K. Devaraj was willing—and now, he is changing the world.

Daily Challenge

With your parents' permission, go to *www.christianservicecharities.org* and read about the many organizations that help people across the world. Is there an organization that makes you think, *I want to do this*? Is there a chance you might have a heart for ministries like these? Pray that God will show you where He wants you to serve Him and help others.

Devo 49

A Big Deal

Read Matthew 14:1–12.

If you poke at a hornet's nest, you should have a really good reason, because you're probably going to get stung.

In today's Bible passage, John the Baptist got stung. No one tells off the king and gets away with it. But John had a really good reason. The king stole his brother's wife, and John knew he had to say something about it. But he paid a deadly price for standing up for God's standards: Herod had John's head chopped off. In the *Odyssey* episodes, "The Big Deal, Parts I and II" (album 35), Aubrey Shepard gets a lead role in a play. Her parents read the play's script and decide Aubrey shouldn't participate. The play attacks Christianity and everything Mr. and Mrs. Shepard believe in. Aubrey doesn't understand what the big deal is. It isn't as if she is agreeing with the lessons of the play. She is just playing a role.

Then Whit sends her to meet John the Baptist in an Imagination Station adventure. John doesn't believe in glossing over sin. He believes everyone should repent of their sin and get ready for Jesus to come—even the king. When Aubrey asks him why he is risking his life to preach his message, John says, "My entire life has been dedicated to the service of God. I answer to Him. I always have. I know of no other way to live than to proclaim God's message." John preaches his message, and he dies for it.

Aubrey decides that holding true to God's standards is actually a big deal.

Are you ever tempted by your friends to do something you know is wrong? Do you stand up to them and say no? Here's the thing about standing up for what you believe in: If you stop doing it, eventually you stop believing it. And if you stop believing it, you begin to make decisions that are going to hurt you. God

Loquacious Learning with Eugene

John the Baptist was only one of many biblical figures who died for the faith. According to church tradition, of the eleven original disciples (minus Judas Iscariot), ten of them were killed for preaching the gospel, including five who were crucified.[1] The apostle John was the only one not put to death directly. Instead, he was exiled to an island by himself.[2] Jesus' disciples were men of conviction, and they should be admired.

doesn't want that. He wants you to believe His Word and stand strong for it, even if it means getting stung. It's a big deal!

Daily Challenge

If you want to stick to something, sometimes it helps to jot things down. Write down one of these sentences: "I will never ______" or "I will always ______." Then make a list of several things you've decided you won't back down from. Keep that list in a safe place. Don't get discouraged if you fail. God forgives. Just keep trying!

Cross-Out Code

Jesus loves us unconditionally. Follow the instructions below to cross off words in the puzzle. Then fill in the remaining words from left to right on the blank lines, starting with the top line, to find out what Matthew 12:50 says about doing God's will.

1. Cross off all names of colors.
2. Cross off all words that begin with C.
3. Cross off all words that begin and end with the same letter.
4. Cross off all words that have a double vowel (as in *seek*).
5. Cross off all words that end with P.
6. Cross off all words that have more than seven letters.

FOR	SEAS	MONUMENT	WHOEVER
CAR	DOES	BLUE	THE
WILL	OF	TAP	TEETH
NOON	STOP	MY	FLUFF
FATHER	CARD	YELLOW	IN
MEEK	HEAVEN	CROSS	GREEN
LOLLIPOP	IS	MY	MOON
HELP	HIGH	BROTHER	PURPLE
AND	SISTER	CLIMB	ROAR
BOOK	ANTELOPE	AND	TROMBONE
MOTHER	RED	FLOOD	CHRISTIAN

________ ________ ________ ________ ________

________ ________ ________ ________ ________

________ ________ ________ ________ ________

________ ________.

Answers on page 209.

Devo 50

God's Math

Read Matthew 14:13–21.

Albert McMakin changed the world. And you've probably never heard of him. As a twenty-four-year-old farmhand, Albert was a new Christian. He loved Jesus and wanted others to know Him too. So when a revival speaker came to Albert's church, he invited as many people as he could—including the sixteen-year-old boy who lived at the farm where Albert worked. The boy wasn't all that interested, but when Albert told him he could drive his old truck, he agreed. And that boy ended up asking Jesus into his life during that week of meeting.[1]

That boy's name was Billy Graham. And he grew up to become the best-known preacher to this day. Millions have gone forward to make a decision for Christ at Mr. Graham's speaking events, and countless others have grown through his radio broadcasts. He's been called the most influential Christian of the twentieth century.

But would that all have happened without Albert McMakin?

It may not have seemed like much to Albert at the time he asked Billy to go to church with him. Just like it might not have seemed like much for that little boy to hand a few fish and some bread over to Jesus. It wasn't much, but God has a way of using even the smallest acts of obedience to do great things.

Did you ever wonder why Jesus didn't just snap his fingers and create a banquet for five thousand people? He could have! He could have turned Peter's sandals into 100-foot long subs or invented pizza delivery right then and there. But he chose to use a little boy's lunch. We don't know that boy's name, but he got to be part of a miracle.

Wandering with Wooton

I was substituting for Whit's Sunday school class and decided we'd reenact the feeding of the five thousand. We went out into the church parking lot, and I took out two cans of tuna fish and five taco shells. (Clearly I need to go grocery shopping.) I started breaking up the shells, talking about how it's not really that much food. It wasn't even enough to feed the thirteen kids in the class. But then these stray cats came around for the tuna, and some birds started swooping down for the taco shells, and that got all the cats kind of excited, so one jumped on my head, trying to catch a bird, and I screamed, and well . . . the food wasn't multiplied, but the chaos was. At least the cats and birds were full afterward.

God wants to use you, too. You might not feel as if you have a lot to give, but don't worry about that. God can multiply what you give in any way He wants. An act of kindness, a few encouraging words to a struggling friend, five dollars from your piggy bank—God can take the smallest gifts and turn them into great things!

Daily Challenge

In your Bible, look up 2 Kings 4:1–7. In this story, how does God use a little to make a lot? What can you give to God that He can turn into something more?

Devo 51

Surfing Boardless

Read Matthew 14:22–36.

Put yourself in Peter's sandals for a minute. Imagine it's you being rocked on a boat in the early morning. Waves slap against the boat as you think about the amazing events of the past few days.

A fellow disciple gasps. "Look!" He points into the mist.

In the dim, hazy light, you see what looks like a white figure coming closer to the boat. You blink a few times . . . Is your mind playing tricks on you? No . . . it *really* is a white figure. A lump forms in your throat. This time Jesus isn't on the boat to help you like last time. Your friends start panicking, sure that it's a ghost or an evil spirit heading their way.

But then you hear a familiar voice. "Take courage. It is I. Don't be afraid."

Take courage! He says, as if He's holding it out to you. As if you could just reach out and grab it.

You lean over the side of the boat. You gaze at this Man who is so much more than a man. You're almost certain He's the Messiah—what else could explain the miracles? With barely a thought, you call back, "If it's you, Lord, tell me to come to you on the water."

"Come," He replies.

You scramble over the edge of the boat and drop into the waves . . . and they hold you.

Those waves, which moments before were so menacing, now feel firm against your sandaled feet. You take one step, then another, then another. The waves splash up against your knees. Your tunic is soaked. A powerful gust of wind comes at you, and you nearly lose your balance. You take another step. But then you lose

Loquacious Learning with Eugene

Take a moment and join me for a brief Greek lesson. The word *courage* that Jesus used in verse 27 comes from the Greek word *tharseō* and refers to "God bolstering the believer, empowering them from within with a bold attitude."[1] I'm very thankful to know that God is the One who gives us faith. It's not something that we need to manufacture ourselves!

sight of Him in the mist, and fear tightens your stomach. What are you doing out here in the middle of wind-tossed waves? *This is crazy! This can't be happening!* The cold waters give way, and you drop into them. Frantically you flail about, trying to find a footing that's no longer there. A wave splashes over your head, and you begin to go under. "Lord, save me!" you cry out.

Immediately, He's there. Taking you by the hand, pulling you out of the water.

Today's Bible passage reminds us that faith isn't a one-time decision. It's a continual choice that takes courage. All too often we limit courage to the bravery associated with putting one's life on the line. The skydiver. The astronaut. The soldier going into battle. But we all have a choice every day to live courageously by faith. To step out of the comfort zone of "our boats" and walk toward Jesus.

With every step Peter took on the water, he had to believe that God was bigger than the waves surrounding him. We need to make those decisions every day, too. It's scary to stand up to the bully who's picking on your friend. It's terrifying to bow your head in prayer before lunch. Perhaps the thought of starting a Bible study ties your stomach in knots. And with each fear comes a question: Is God bigger than whatever I'm afraid of? The answer is always yes.

Daily Challenge

Write your own story about steps of faith you've taken toward Jesus. Include any doubts or fears you may have experienced—that's part of Peter's story, too!

Devo 52

A Matter of the Heart

Read Matthew 15:1–20.

If you were on a mission, sent by God to tell people about Him, where would you look for assistants to help you? Would you go to churches to find religious leaders who are well versed in the Scriptures and have been following God's laws since their youth? Or would you check out the lake, where common, uneducated fishermen hang out with big nets?

Jesus went to the lake to find men to help Him in His ministry. Can you imagine what it would have been like if Jesus had chosen the Pharisees to be His disciples?

"Uh, Jesus . . . sorry to mention this, but we really shouldn't be raising people from the dead today. It's the Sabbath."

"I'm sorry, Jesus, but did you just touch that man with leprosy? Oh, boy, you have some serious ceremonial hand washing to do when we get back to the temple."

"Does that bread you just used to feed five thousand hungry people have yeast in it? I'm gonna have to report you to the chief priest . . ."

Why did Jesus pick fishermen and other common people to be His followers instead of religious leaders? Because He knew everyone's hearts. He knew that Peter, John, and James would eventually become ten times more godly as leaders than any of the Pharisees. The Pharisees had hearts only for themselves. The disciples had hearts for God and for others.

First Corinthians 13:3 says, "If I give all I possess to the poor . . . but have not love, I gain nothing." God doesn't look at all of our accomplishments when He

Whit's Wisdom

Jesus used a religious leader to spread the good news. Saul was a member of the Sanhedrin, a religious group who persecuted and killed people who preached about Jesus. Of course, before Jesus could use Saul, He had to completely change Saul into a true man of God. Saul's name was also changed to a Roman name, Paul. He became perhaps the greatest Christian missionary who ever lived. He is a testimony to the life-changing power of Jesus.

chooses us to follow Him. He looks at the heart. Do you have a love for Jesus and others? If you do, you are the perfect person to join Him on His mission to save the world.

Daily Challenge

Share love with a neighbor or a family member by secretly doing something for him or her. Clean your brother's room while he's gone. Make an encouraging card for someone and leave it on his or her doorstep. Leave candy or cookies on your teacher's desk when she's out.

Devo 53

God Loves Them?!

Read Matthew 15:21–39.

What do you think of this list of people?

Pharisees. Rude waiters. Children who block your way because they're trying to go up the down escalator. Crabby neighbors. Teachers who stand behind you in the school cafeteria to make sure you eat your peaches. Your annoying little brother who stuffs your LEGOs up his nose. The guy next door who plays bagpipes at four o'clock in the morning. Liars. Murderers. Thieves.

So what do you think this is a list of? Annoying people? People you dislike? Guess what? It's also a list of the people Jesus died for on the cross. The verse that starts "God loved the world so much . . ." (John 3:16, NIRV)—well, the bagpipe guy is part of that world. Jesus loves the bagpipe guy.

When Jesus was on the earth, most people believed He came to save only one group of people—the Jews. In fact, when a woman came to Him for help (a woman who wasn't a Jew), Jesus tested her faith in Him by saying, "I was sent only to the lost sheep of Israel [the Jews]" (Matthew 15:24). The woman passed the faith test by believing He cared even though she wasn't Jewish, and, of course, Jesus helped her. And then, as if that wasn't enough proof that He came for everyone, He went and fed four thousand hungry strangers.

How do we act toward people we don't like? Do we ignore them? Make fun of them? Do we laugh when they fail? The next time you feel like laughing at someone, remember that Jesus died for that person, too. Jesus loves everyone. If that person fell into the mud, Jesus wouldn't be laughing with you. He would be lending a hand to help him or her out of the mud. Love others no matter who they are or which way they're going on the escalator.

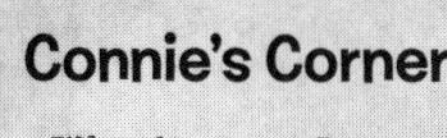

Connie's Corner

I'll admit it—I went through a donut phase. I bought a donut every morning. Yes, I know they're bad for you. I got reminded every morning when I went to the donut shop and the guy behind the counter looked at me like I was poisoning myself with fried sugar. It got to the point where I couldn't stand that guy, and I gave him ugly looks every day so that he knew I didn't like him. Then one Sunday I saw him at church. Oops. I was embarrassed that I had treated him so badly. Jesus loves him, too.

Daily Challenge

Make a list of two or three people you really don't like. Then do something nice for them and watch their reactions. Who knows? Maybe you'll make a new friend!

Devo 54

Moldy Bread

Read Matthew 16:1–12.

There is a community project in England where prisoners put on stage plays to teach young children about the dangers of crime. After the shows, the prisoners lead a question-and-answer time. During one of these Q and A's, a man named Frazer answered a question. Frazer is serving ten years in prison for dealing drugs. He said this: "I've learned how small crimes lead to bigger ones. I started stealing sweets from a shop; I wasn't even ten years old. Why? I did it because my friends would say, 'Come on—Go and get some Yorkie [candy] Bars, mate,' and I did. Only twenty years later I wish I had just turned round and said no! But that was the start of things."[1]

A candy bar eventually would send Frazer to jail for ten years. But what does a candy bar have to do with selling drugs? Because once a sin begins to take hold in your life, it will lead to bigger sins. Frazer decided at ten that stealing wasn't such a bad thing. And look where it got him.

In today's Bible passage, Jesus was talking about yeast. Earlier we read that He talked about yeast being like the kingdom of heaven. Now He was telling the disciples to avoid the yeast of the Pharisees. In this chapter, yeast is referring to the teaching of the Pharisees. So which is it? Is yeast good or bad?

Actually, it can be both. Yeast is very small, but when it's added to flour, the flour rises and becomes a loaf of bread. Yeast releases a gas that makes the bread dough grow bigger.[2]

The kingdom of heaven becoming bigger is a good thing. But the false teachings of the Pharisees becoming bigger is a bad thing. So this is what Jesus was

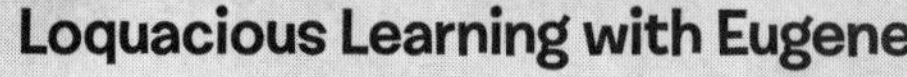

Loquacious Learning with Eugene

Yeast is the ingredient that is used to make most bread light and fluffy. Many don't know that yeast is actually a living organism. But this organism doesn't grow to make bread rise. In fact, when bread is baked, the yeast feeds on sugar in the bread and releases carbon dioxide. The carbon dioxide bubbles make the bread grow. This is roughly analogous to the way sin works. Sin starts small on the inside. Sometimes others can't see it. But slowly it grows inside you like carbon-dioxide bubbles in bread. The only way to keep it from growing is to turn off the oven and take out the bread.[3]

warning the disciples about. If the disciples began to believe the lies of the Pharisees, those lies would grow inside them and infect them. In the same way, if you listen to wrong teaching, eventually, it can make you doubt the teachings of Jesus, and it can lead you into sin. And we all know that little sins lead to bigger sins, as Frazer learned. So the best thing to do when you're tempted by sin is what Frazer admits he should've done twenty years ago. Say no!

Daily Challenge

Think and pray about any "little white lies" you've told in the past few days. Or a very small thing you took that wasn't yours. Or that moment of time when you had a thought you shouldn't have had. Confess those "small" sins and ask God to help you not to give in.

Devo 55

The Pop Quiz

Read Matthew 16:13–28; 17:22–23; 20:17–19.

Peter must have felt good about himself when Jesus praised him for answering His question correctly: "Who do you say I am?"

Peter replied, "You are the Christ [the Messiah], the Son of the living God" (Matthew 16:15–16).

Ding, ding, ding! Jesus loved that answer. But then Jesus began telling His friends about what was about to happen to Him. Hard stuff. He told them He was going to suffer and be mocked, betrayed, and killed by the Jews who hated Him. Peter, thinking he was on a roll, said, "No! That's impossible! I won't let it happen!"

But Jesus took the wind out of Peter's sails. He responded to Peter with anger. How dare Peter try to get in the way of God's ultimate plan to save the world!

It wasn't that Jesus didn't appreciate that Peter cared so much for him. Jesus' point was that if Peter was going to call Jesus his Savior, he needed to accept the difficult things that were part of following Jesus. Not just the good or easy things.

At this point the disciples were probably thinking that Jesus was getting ready to overthrow the government and take over like Superman beating up a gang of ninjas. But God's plans for Jesus were different. God's will was for Jesus to die on a cross to save the world.

The question Jesus asked His disciples is a question we have to answer too. Who is Jesus to you? If you say, "My Savior," then you have to accept the hard stuff as well as the good stuff. The hard stuff is, well, hard. Giving up complete control of your life to God is hard. Standing up for what's right is hard. Resisting temptation is hard. But the good stuff is really, really good. It includes a God who is with

Whit's Wisdom

It must have been quite a shock for the disciples when Jesus told them that He was going to die soon. This was the first time Jesus mentioned that He was going to be crucified. And Jesus talked about it a lot in the weeks that followed. Yet when it all actually happened, the disciples still didn't seem quite ready for it. In fact, it wasn't until Jesus had already gone back to heaven that they finally "got it." It's good to know that God has patience with us as we try to understand what it means to follow Him.

you twenty-four hours a day and promises to guide you. It also includes being used by God to help change the world, not to mention a ticket to heaven.

So here's your pop quiz: Who do you say Jesus is?

Daily Challenge

Who is Jesus to you? Write it down or tell a parent, friend, or sibling.

Devo 56

In His Presence

Read Matthew 17:1–13.

Say you're walking through the mall, and suddenly the queen of England comes out of the Sunglasses Barn. What do you do? There are rules about addressing the queen, and you certainly don't want her to be upset with you for being impolite. Well, worry no more. Here are some official rules to help you in case that ever happens:

1. Greet her as "Your Majesty" at first, and then after that use "Ma'am."
2. If you're not British, don't curtsy or bow. You can nod your head if you want.
3. Don't extend your hand to shake her hand unless she offers her hand first.
4. No hugs. No kisses. And don't call her by her first name. Or Queenie. Or the Big Q.
5. If you don't have a British accent, don't fake it to sound like her. That's just silly.[1]

Have you ever thought about what it will be like when you go to heaven and see Jesus in person for the first time? Won't that be amazing? What do you think your response will be? Tears? Laughter? Joy? If you're anything like the disciples, it will be awe. You will be amazed at His presence.

In today's Bible passage, Peter, James, and John went with Jesus to the top of a mountain. There they saw Jesus' appearance suddenly change. Jesus' face was radiant like the sun, and his clothes shone like white lightening as He spoke with Moses and Elijah, who had come down from heaven. Peter probably didn't know what to do, so his response was the most natural thing that came to him: worship.

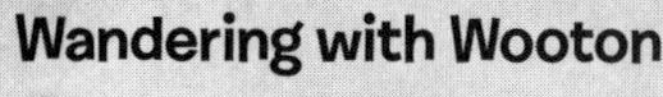

Wandering with Wooton

One time I met one of my heroes. Irwin Masters, the man who created the Tarantula Man comic-book series, came to Holstein's Books in Odyssey. I was so nervous that I ended up trapping his legs under an entire shelf of health-and-wellness books. Long story. I left there disappointed. He was a little angry with me (of course, he was trapped under a bookcase at the time). It's going to be a lot different when I meet Jesus for the first time, because I know He loves me, even if I do accidentally drop something heavy on Him.

That will probably be the natural response for us, too, when we see Jesus in person. We will probably fall to our knees in worship as we gaze upon His glory and greatness.

While we're here on earth, we should practice worshipping Jesus by coming before Him in prayer in the same way. We should humble ourselves every day and thank God for His power and love. God is holy, awesome, and worthy of our worship, no matter where we are.

Daily Challenge

Start your prayer today with a whole lot of worship. Sing a praise song to Jesus. Thank Him for all the things He is to you. Thank Him for all the things He's given you and done for you.

Names of Jesus

When Jesus asked Peter, "Who do you say I am?" Peter replied, "You are the Christ, the Son of the living God" (Matthew 16:15-16). Cross out every Q, X, Z, J, and B to find ten more names or words that describe who Jesus is. The names can appear frontward, backward, up, down, or diagonally. Then write those names on the lines provided.

X	J	Q	D	Q	B	J	J	Z	X	B
Q	B	R	Z	J	X	Q	S	B	J	L
G	O	D	A	N	D	M	A	N	Q	E
L	Z	C	Z	J	B	X	V	Q	B	U
X	B	Q	A	X	Q	K	I	N	G	N
S	J	Z	B	R	B	J	O	Q	Z	A
H	Q	X	Z	Q	P	Z	R	X	Q	M
E	T	E	A	C	H	E	R	Z	B	M
P	J	Z	Q	Z	L	X	N	J	Z	I
H	Q	B	X	A	J	B	B	T	J	X
E	Z	J	E	Q	Z	Q	X	J	E	Q
R	X	H	J	B	X	B	Q	Z	B	R
D	F	R	I	E	N	D	J	B	X	Q

Answers on page 210.

Devo 57

A Seed of Faith

Read Matthew 17:14–21.

The *Odyssey* episode "When in Doubt . . . Pray!" (album 30) features a true story about a faith-filled man named George Mueller. He operates an orphanage in Bristol, England, in the 1800s. Almost every week the orphanage runs low on food. So Mueller and the children pray that God will provide something for the next day.

One night the children go to bed with no food in any of the cupboards. So the children sleep, not knowing if there will be breakfast on the table the next morning. Sunrise comes, and still there is no food. When the children appear for breakfast, Mueller has them sit at the empty table. Then he begins to pray, thanking God for the food He is going to provide.

A few minutes later, there is a knock on the door. It is a local baker, who tells Mueller that he couldn't sleep the night before. He'd had a strong feeling that he was supposed to bake bread for the orphanage. He brings in the loaves he had baked for the children, and they pile all the loaves on the table.

A short time later, a delivery man knocks on the door. He has been delivering milk, but his wagon is broken down. He has to take the wagon in for repairs, but he needs to get rid of the milk first. Would Mueller's orphanage like the milk? he asks.

That morning the children have milk and bread for breakfast. God provided for their needs just as Mueller said He would.

George Mueller had great faith in God. But do you think he always did? Probably not. Like the rest of us, he probably found that his faith was small and weak at times. But as he prayed and trusted God, God began answering his prayers.

Connie's Corner

Sometimes it bugs me when I see how much faith Whit has. One time there was a huge storm in Odyssey, and Whit and I were the only ones at Whit's End. The front window broke, and Whit got pieces of glass in his leg. I was freaking out! But Whit stayed calm and started saying Bible verses. I was amazed at his faith and wondered if I could ever have faith that strong. God did protect us, and Whit was all right. I'm so glad Jesus talked about people with a small amount of faith being able to do great things, because He was talking about me!

Soon Mueller was able to go to bed at night believing in his heart that God would put food on the table the next morning. That's how "faith as small as a mustard seed" can move mountains (Matthew 17:20).

God may not always answer your prayers exactly the way you want Him to. But He always wants the best for you. He cares about you and knows what you need in every situation.

Like George Mueller, keep praying and trusting that God will take care of you!

Daily Challenge

Follow George Mueller's example and take a step of faith today. There are countless ways you can trust God to provide for your needs and the needs of others. One way might be to give money to your church when you have very little to give. Or you could help someone you think will reject you. Or you could spend time with God, trusting Him to help you find the time to get other things done.

Devo 58

Marie, the Supervillain

Read Matthew 17:24–27.

Jennifer pounded the top of her dresser, rattling the hamster cage. The hamster poked his nose out of the toilet-paper roll to see what was going on. Jennifer's older sister, Marie, had done it this time. It was the final straw, and Jennifer wasn't going to take it anymore.

She thought about what she should do. First, she decided to look up attorneys on the Internet and call a lawyer. She wanted to sue her sister for more money than she could pay in a thousand lifetimes. Then Jennifer took all her savings and rented a huge billboard that everyone could see on the highway. She put a picture of Marie on it, with two words at the bottom—BAD SISTER.

Marie came home after school, and Jennifer glared at her. Fuming, Jennifer said, "You wore my coat this morning."

Marie said, "Oh. Sorry. I guess I grabbed the wrong one."

Jennifer gulped. "Excuse me. I need to go to the highway to take something down."

Jennifer overreacted, didn't she? But don't we do this sometimes too? We get mad at each other over silly little things that don't matter.

Today's Scripture passage shows us that even Jesus picked His battles. It didn't make sense for Him to pay the temple tax. It would have been like a king taxing his own children. Since God is the true King, why would His Son pay a tax to the church? But Jesus didn't figure this was a battle worth fighting. So He sent Peter on a mission to find money for the tax inside a fish! This is one of the coolest miracles in the Bible!

Loquacious Learning with Eugene

Journalist Sydney J. Harris once said, "If a small thing has the power to make you angry, does that not indicate something about your size?" The implication in his quote is that only lesser people get angry over insignificant things. While there is some truth in this statement, it is not entirely accurate. There is a time and place for anger, as evidenced by the righteous anger Jesus expressed in the Bible. The key is to use anger wisely and in a God-honoring way.

Ask God to help you understand the difference between important and unimportant things. Important things are worth caring about, and unimportant things are worth letting go. If a friend uses your stuff without your permission, is it really a big deal? Just ask him or her politely not to do it again if it really bothers you. If your brother gets more Christmas presents than you, does it really matter? Plenty of things in life are worth caring about. But there's no need to get upset or lose your temper over little things that don't really matter.

Daily Challenge

Recall a few times when you got angry with someone over a silly or insignificant thing. Go to that person and ask forgiveness for making such a big deal out of it. And ask God to help you keep your temper under control.

Devo 59

Like a Child

Read Matthew 18:1–6; 19:13–15.

A Japanese folktale tells about a boy who dreamed of becoming a skilled swordsman. So he went to the greatest instructor in the land and asked the man to be his teacher. The teacher said, "You must do everything I ask without question." The boy agreed without hesitation.

The teacher first instructed his student to go to the school and walk along the edge of the floor mat. The boy was told to put one foot directly in front of the other, like walking on a balance beam. So the boy went to the school and walked back and forth on the mat. "This is ridiculous!" he said to himself. "How is this going to help me wield a sword?" Then he sat down and refused to do the exercise anymore.

Every day the teacher gave him the same instruction to walk along the floor mat. Every day the boy went to the school and did nothing but pout.

Finally the boy went to his teacher and asked, "When are we going to start learning to use the sword?" The teacher asked him if he had walked along the floor mat every day. The boy lied and said yes.

The teacher decided the boy was ready for the next lesson. He told his student that the teaching would take place at the top of a mountain.

On the way up the mountain, the teacher and his student encountered a deep gorge with jagged rocks and rushing water below. The only way to the other side was to walk across a narrow fallen tree. The boy hesitated, but the teacher said, "It is wider than the floor mat at school. You should have no trouble crossing."

The boy slowly started across the gorge, but halfway to the other side, he lost

Whit's Wisdom

The hymn "Jesus Loves the Little Children" was written by a preacher named C. Herbert Woolston. In church we often just sing the chorus, but the song actually has three verses. One of them says, "I will take you by the hand / Lead you to the better land / Jesus loves the little children of the world."[2] Jesus certainly did love children. He asked them to come to Him several times. My guess is that those little children loved Jesus too.

his balance and fell into the river. The teacher rescued him and pulled him ashore. Then he asked the boy, "How will you learn the sword when you haven't even learned to walk?"[1]

In today's Scripture passage, Jesus told His disciples that the greatest in the kingdom of heaven would be like little children—humble. Prideful people will reject God's instructions. Only those with childlike faith will admit that they're not as smart as God and will do what He says.

Daily Challenge

Go through the book of Proverbs in your Bible and find some verses on humility or pride. There are tons, especially in chapters 3 and 25–27. After you've read through these proverbs, pray and ask God for a humble heart.

Devo 60

Ready to Run

Read Matthew 18:7–9.

What would you do in each of these scenarios?

1. You're hiking in the woods, and someone runs past you screaming that a bear is coming your way. Would you . . .
    a. run away from the bear as fast as you can?
    b. stay where you are and drink some orange juice?
    c. try to get as close to the bear as you can without being mauled?
2. You're outside, and you see a tornado coming your way. Would you . . .
    a. go inside your house and take cover in the basement?
    b. sit down and have a granola bar?
    c. run in the direction of the funnel cloud and try to dodge it if it gets too close?
3. You notice a large beehive in your backyard tree, and several bees are swarming around it. Would you . . .
    a. go inside to tell your mom about it?
    b. sit there and watch the bees?
    c. climb up the tree with a piece of toast to get some free honey?

Most of us would agree that "a" is the wisest response in each scenario. A "b" response isn't very wise, but by far, the most foolish response is "c." In fact, you might be wondering why anyone would choose "c" in any scenario.

But the truth is, we often do very foolish things when it comes to temptation. We make choices that bring us dangerously close to sinning. We may think we're safe because we don't plan on doing anything wrong. Or we may think we're strong enough to resist temptation. For example, you might go to a movie

Connie's Corner

For a long time I subscribed to fashion magazines and loved to flip through them. But it seemed like I always ended up buying more clothes at the end of the day. Or I'd look at the models and start feeling sad because I wasn't pretty enough. I thought I could keep getting the magazines and ignore those feelings—but it didn't work that way. It wasn't until I canceled my subscriptions and avoided the temptation to read the magazines altogether that I was finally able to stop struggling with those thoughts.

with bad language and violence because you think, *I'll just ignore those parts. It won't affect me.* Or you might choose to hang out with a friend who always gets in trouble because you believe, *I won't get in trouble. I'm too strong to be influenced by my friend's behavior.*

The *Odyssey* episode "B-TV: Temptation" (album 49) includes a sketch about Joseph and how he avoided temptation. He ran in the other direction! That's how we should respond to temptation too.

In today's Scripture reading, Jesus said some pretty drastic things. Does He really want us to gouge out our eyes and cut off our hands because they cause us to sin? If that were true, most people would be running around with a missing eye or hand. But Jesus knew that our eyes and hands don't make us sin. We sin because our hearts give in to temptation. Jesus used this illustration to make a point. He was encouraging His followers to make radical decisions to avoid temptation. That's still great advice to follow today!

Daily Challenge

Think about choices you've made that brought you closer to temptation and sin. When are you most tempted to do things that are wrong? List some ways you can avoid those situations.

Devo 61

One Little Sheep

Read Matthew 18:10–14.

Job description for position of shepherd:

1. Must keep track of sheep and know each of them by name.
2. Must care for sheep both day and night.
3. Must sleep at gate of pen with staff in hand to ward off wolves and other predators.
4. Must help sheep get up if they fall. Their wool is so heavy, they're unable to get up on their own.
5. Must check sheep at the end of every day for any wounds and bandage them up.
6. Must lead sheep to clean water and fresh grass on a daily basis.
7. Must wait for sheep patiently because they can be very slow.[1]

The Bible often refers to us as sheep and God as our Shepherd. In biblical times, people were familiar with the life of a shepherd. They knew that good shepherds cared deeply for their sheep and met all the "requirements" of their job description.

Jesus told the parable of the lost sheep to show how much He cares for us. If even *one* of us wanders off, He'll come looking for that lost sheep. We're that important to Him.

In the *Odyssey* episode "A Lesson from Mike" (album 31), Julie hears about a boy in her school who died in a tragic accident. Even though Mike wasn't her friend, Julie feels compelled to learn more about him. She discovers that she and Mike had a lot in common. They could have been good friends if she'd gotten to know him earlier.

Just like Mike, every person God created has incredible value. He made all of us in His image. And He gave each of us unique gifts and a special calling. Follow-

Whit's Wisdom

I love this C. S. Lewis quote: "You have never talked to a mere mortal."[2] It's a great reminder that every human being is significant and of great value in God's sight. No one should be overlooked. Sometimes we need to remember that every person we meet was created by God for His glory.

ing are a few reminders of how valuable you are to God. (Look up these verses in your Bible to get the full picture.)

- *Psalm 139* says that God made you wonderfully, that He wrote down all your days in His book before you were even born, and that He knows all your thoughts.
- *Colossians 3:12* says you are chosen and dearly loved by God.
- *Matthew 10:29–31* says that God knows the number of hairs on your head.
- *Zephaniah 3:17* says that God takes great delight in you and rejoices over you.
- *Ephesians 3:16–21* says you can't even comprehend how big God's love is for you.

And that's only a small picture of how much Jesus values you. He not only loves you the way He loves all people, but He also loves *you* individually. He designed you before birth, has gifted you in unique ways, and has given you a special calling in life. You can't possibly measure God's love for you. It's way beyond anything you can imagine!

Daily Challenge

Memorize one of the Bible verses in this devo. Quote it to yourself when you begin to question your worth or the worth of others.

Devo 62

The Value of Friendship

Read Matthew 18:15–20.

Relationships are important, but they aren't always easy. People make mistakes—they hurt our feelings, break promises, or forget birthdays. Sometimes it's easier to just be by ourselves. But that's not the way God designed us. Flaws and all, He created us to need one another.

In today's Scripture passage, God talks about the ups and downs of relationships. The downside is that sometimes friends mess up. For example, let's say a kid named Andrew saw his friend Luke take money out of the youth-group collection plate.

"It's for the needy," Luke said, "and I *need* a new skateboard." Luke chuckled at his own words as he stuffed the bills into his pocket.

If you were Andrew, what would your next step be according to Matthew 18?

a. Go tell your pastor what Luke did.
b. Send out a mass e-mail telling everyone you know that Luke's a thief.
c. Go to Luke one-on-one and explain why his behavior was wrong and encourage him to make it right.
d. Ignore the issue completely. It's none of your business. And it wasn't *that* much money.
e. Don't say anything to Luke, but call another friend when you get home and say, "You won't believe what Luke did!"

The correct answer is, of course, "c."

Sometimes we have arguments with our friends not because they've done anything wrong but because we just disagree. In the *Odyssey* episode "Red Wagons and Pink Flamingos" (album 22), Erica and her good friend Kim get into a big

Wandering with Wooton

My twin brother, Wellington, and I don't always get along. He didn't like the cauliflower-cocoa cake I made him for our birthday (even after I told him the health benefits of cauliflower). And he *really* didn't appreciate it when I put Jell-O in his showerhead and turned his hair green. I was really young (like twenty-two), so I don't know why he got so mad. But even if he doesn't always get my sense of humor or my silly pranks, he's still my brother. So I try to apologize when I do things that annoy him. Which, as you can see, is pretty much all the time.

fight that nearly ends their friendship. But Erica is reminded that friendship is more valuable than winning an argument. Friendship is worth fighting for.

Because friendships are so important, Jesus outlined a way for us to deal with disagreements. He knows how easy it is for us to respond out of anger or fear or jealousy. But God values friendships and doesn't want us to handle them carelessly.

Daily Challenge

Jesus said that when we gather to pray, God is with us and will answer our prayers. Get together with some friends from church to pray together, even if it's just for a few minutes. Maybe you have an unsaved friend you want to pray for, or you have some other prayer requests. Praying together is a powerful thing!

Devo 63

Grudge Not, Lest You Be Grudged

Read Matthew 18:21–35.

In 2003, three houses in Waukesha, Wisconsin, were vandalized. Words had been spray-painted on the houses and the cars. Potted plants had been knocked over. Tires had been slashed. Police soon figured out that all these crimes had been committed by the same man—Matthew Mundschau.

What had these people done to Matthew? Well, as it turned out, nothing lately. Matthew later explained to police that he had made a list of three people who had wronged him over the past ten years. He had been waiting years for just the right moment to get even.

One victim was responsible for Mundschau getting fired from a supermarket job ten years earlier. Another victim had stepped in to stop an argument Mundschau was having with someone. And one woman had simply cut him off in traffic. Mundschau got the addresses of these people and began to get his revenge.[1]

Okay, Matthew Mundschau was a bit of a nut. But don't we all hold grudges against those who hurt us? Don't we love getting even? Don't we love saying, "Yeah, but three weeks ago, you did this . . ." Even after people say they're sorry and ask forgiveness, we love bringing up the bad stuff again later on.

There are two problems with grudges. First, they hurt us more than the people who wrong us. Anne Lamott says, "Not forgiving is like drinking rat poison and then waiting for the rat to die."[2] Second, when we hold a grudge, we're ignoring what God has done for us. When we ask God for forgiveness, He does it freely. We sin against Him every day, and yet He is always quick to forgive. He doesn't hold grudges; He just forgives. When we hold grudges, we've decided not

Connie's Corner

One time at a restaurant, a waiter wouldn't let me use a coupon because it had expired. I was so mad that I gave him a bad tip. But then, after dinner, he ran outside in the rain to return the jacket I'd left at the table. I felt bad. It was really nice of him, not just because he ran out in the rain, but because he forgave me for giving him a bad tip. It made me want to forgive faster . . . and eat at that restaurant again so I could give him a huge tip.

to forgive, even though God has forgiven all of our sins. How many times should we forgive? "Seventy times seven" (Matthew 18:22, NKJV)—or in other words, as many times as God has forgiven us.

Guess what? You'll never outdo God when it comes to forgiving.

Daily Challenge

Think of someone who has wronged you during the past week. Have you forgiven that person? Or are you still holding a grudge? Now think of all the sins you've committed in the past week. If you asked God to forgive your sins, did He? Hint: Yes.

Scrambled Surprise

1. Famous missionary who prayed for food for orphans. (Devo 57)

   O E G R G E   R L E U M E L

   __ __ __ __ __ __   __ __ __ __ __ __ __

2. It's good to let these types of things go so they don't make you angry. (Devo 58)

   N M O T N U I P R A T

   __ __ __ __ __ __ __ __ __ __ __

3. Keep this under control. (Devo 58)

   P T E E M R

   __ __ __ __ __ __

4. Prideful people reject God's ____. (Devo 59)

   S O T U T N I S R C I N

   __ __ __ __ __ __ __ __ __ __ __ __

5. When we experience this, we should run. (Devo 60)

   N T E O M I P T T A

   __ __ __ __ __ __ __ __ __ __

6. A famous Bible person who avoided temptation. (Devo 60; Genesis 39)

   S E O P H J

   __ __ __ __ __ __

7. The Bible often refers to God as being our ____. (Devo 61)

   P E E H S D R H

   __ __ __ __ __ __ __ __

8. In the Odyssey episode "Red Wagons and Pink Flamingos," Erica and Kim get into a big fight that nearly ends their ____ . (Devo 62)

   R S P N I I H F E D

   __ __ __ __ __ __ __ __ __ __

9. How many times should we forgive? (Devo 63; Matthew 18:22, NKJV)

   Y S T E V N E S T E I M

   __ __ __ __ __ __ __ __ __ __ __ __

   N S E E V

   __ __ __ __ __

10. God doesn't hold these. (Devo 63)

    D E G G R S U

    __ __ __ __ __ __ __

Answers on page 210.

Devo 64

Like Chocolate Milk

Read Matthew 19:1–12.

Donna Barclay had never heard her parents argue so loudly before.

In the *Odyssey* episode "The Vow" (album 9), Donna worries that her parents might be getting a divorce. In fact, her friend's parents were getting a divorce, and the signs were the same—including the heated arguments. Donna and her brother, Jimmy, come up with a plan to get their parents to sign a contract promising they will stay together.

Mr. and Mrs. Barclay assure their children that the arguments aren't a signal that they are on the verge of divorce. In fact, they say, disagreeing and coming to a solution together is a sign of a healthy marriage. But most important, the Barclays say they don't need a written contract to keep them together. They are bound together by an even better agreement called marriage. The Barclays made a covenant with each other in front of God. And it's one promise they intend to keep.

God loves marriage. His perfect plan is that when a man and a woman get married, they'll stay together forever. In fact, God thinks so much of marriage that He says married couples aren't just two people anymore—they become one.

Once you put chocolate powder in milk, you can no longer separate the two. They are no longer just chocolate and milk. They become chocolate milk. In the same way, two married people become one unit, and that unit should never be divided.

God created us for relationship and designed marriage so we wouldn't have to live alone. That's why He gave Adam a partner in the garden of Eden. Eve became Adam's wife. They got into trouble, made mistakes, and were punished for dis-

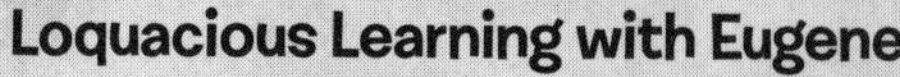

Loquacious Learning with Eugene

Compared to fifty years ago in the United States, adults are 21 percent less likely to be married, and divorces are more than twice as common.[1] These are certainly startling statistics, but that shouldn't change our view of the importance of marriage. My wife, Katrina, and I believed when we got married that it was a promise we were making not only to each other but also to God. We also believed that our marriage bond would never be broken. God doesn't want us to become a bad statistic. He wants us to have a holy marriage.

obeying God. But in spite of all that, they stayed together under the covenant God established for them.

At the end of the *Odyssey* episode, Donna and Jimmy watch as their parents renew their vows in front of them. Mr. and Mrs. Barclay probably didn't need to do this. Their original vows will last them a lifetime.

Daily Challenge

Ask your parents how they met or about their first date. Then ask other questions you may have about their relationship. Your parents might even give you some great advice about how to prepare for marriage.

Devo 65

Can't Buy Me Eternity

Read Matthew 19:16–30.

Lenny had everything. His father was a wealthy businessman, and Lenny never had a single need in his life. He had the best toys growing up, ate the most delicious foods, and wore the finest clothing. Everyone admired and respected him not because he was particularly talented or smart but because he was rich. Aware of this, Lenny enjoyed showing everyone how rich he was.

One day Lenny's father died suddenly. Lenny was surprised when almost no one showed up for the funeral. The funeral was beautiful, of course, with the most expensive casket and flower arrangements. However, Lenny noticed that his mother had paid for all the flowers. This made Lenny think about real life. Was there more to life than just living well? Had his father made a difference? Lenny wondered if *he* made any difference. What would happen to him after he died?

Lenny had heard about a wise man who roamed about in a town nearby. So he went to ask the man a question: "What do I need to do to inherit eternal life?"

The wise man, named Jesus, said, "Go, sell your possessions and give to the poor" (Matthew 19:21).

Lenny was not only shocked at the answer; he was in utter dismay. Give up his wealth? How could he do that? Lenny walked away, not ready to give up the best toys, the most delicious foods, and the finest clothing.

Jesus told His disciples that it's hard for a rich man to get into heaven. But it's not because he's wealthy; it's because it's difficult for a wealthy person to put God first. In fact, Jesus said that it's "easier for a camel to go through the eye of a needle than for a rich man to enter the kingdom of God" (verse 24). His point was that it's impossible for us to save ourselves or buy our way into heaven. "But

Wandering with Wooton

One month I decided to keep track of how I used each hour of my day. If I took out the time I spent sleeping, eating, delivering mail, and driving, I figured out that 48 percent of my time was spent with my friends, 24 percent cooking and cleaning, 16 percent watching TV, 7 percent doing licorice-based art, 3 percent practicing lumber sports, and 2 percent spending time with God. I decided that was really messed up, so the next month I cut back on TV and licorice art. Oh, and cleaning. The extra time I spent with God was great!

with God all things are possible" (verse 26). And with His help, we can put Him first in our lives.

Besides possessions, what other things do we put before God? Our time? Our friends? Our popularity? Our toys?

Missionary Jim Elliot said, "He is no fool who gives what he cannot keep to gain what he cannot lose."[1] Money will fade away someday. Jesus will not.

Daily Challenge

Do what Wooton did and keep track of how you spend your time for a few days. Is anything out of whack? What practical steps can you take to put God first in your life and spend more time with Him?

Devo 66

The Cooler Side of Heaven

Read Matthew 20:1–16.

Once there were two men. The first was a missionary who spread the good news of Jesus to thousands of people in the jungles of South America throughout his lifetime. The second was a lifelong criminal who spent his last twenty years in prison. When he got sick and realized he was going to die, he asked for a pastor to come to his cell and tell him about Jesus. The man accepted Jesus as his Savior just a few days before he died.

What's the difference between these two men? Do you think the first will get deluxe accommodations in heaven—a mansion of gold, crystal chandeliers adorning every room, and live swans gracing the glittering pools?

And the second man? Maybe he'll be sent to the outskirts of heaven—right outside the city-limit sign. In that part of town, the golden streets are kind of dingy, and the singing angels are a bit off-key.

But Jesus said no. According to His parable about the vineyard workers, the ones who came at the beginning of the day received the same wage as the people who were only there a few hours. We don't know much about what heaven is going to be like, but this parable teaches us that both the missionary and the prisoner are welcome.

The same reward of salvation is available to everyone—young or old, bad or good, pretty or plain. God doesn't look at age, gender, nationality, color, or income level to determine who gets into heaven. When you accept Jesus as your Savior, you're on the list. Period.

Remember this the next time you wonder about the bully who treats you

Connie's Corner

My great uncle Joe was really old before he asked Jesus to be his Savior. I asked Uncle Joe to come to church with me all the time, and he kept saying no. He said church was for younger people. He thought that it was too late for him to make a change in his life. But Whit and I explained the parable of the workers to him—where the master paid all the workers the same wage no matter how long they worked for him. I told Uncle Joe that Jesus was calling him right then and there. When Joe asked Jesus into his heart, it was a great moment!

so meanly. Yes, Jesus came to save him, too. What about the criminal who keeps breaking the law and ending up back in jail? He isn't outside of the grasp of Jesus' loving hand either. And the friend who says she hates church and everything to do with God? Jesus says, "Come." He came for us all.

Daily Challenge

Pray for several people who seem far away from God right now, even if it seems impossible for them to know Jesus. Remember Matthew 19:26 from yesterday's devotion: "With God, all things are possible."

Devo 67

Looking Out for Number Three

Read Matthew 20:20–34.

A famous philosopher named Robert Nozick came up with an idea called "the experience machine" in 1974. The idea was that you could plug into this machine and experience only pleasure. If you plugged in, you would be happy all the time. You would never be sad, bored, or hungry. Would you plug into the machine? If you did, how long would you stay there? Would you ever go back to the way things were?[1]

Jesus would probably think this is a ridiculous question. We weren't put on earth to make ourselves happy. And yet our culture tells us over and over to do just that. (Making ourselves happy usually involves buying something.)

Consider this popular saying: "I'm looking out for number one." It means you're number one—you're putting yourself first. You're going to do things that serve yourself, not others.

In today's Scripture passage, the mother of brothers James and John asked Jesus if her boys could be His right-hand men in His kingdom. Jesus couldn't believe that they missed the point of His ministry completely. Jesus didn't come to be served. He came to serve others. And that's our job, too. We're here to put others before ourselves.

After Jesus said this to James and John, two blind men approached Him and asked for healing. Perhaps Jesus looked at James and John right before He touched the blind men's eyes—as if to say, "Watch and learn. This is how you serve others." Jesus gave the two men their sight. He responded to their needs just like a good servant does.

Whit's Wisdom

Jesus had many great sayings. Three of my favorites are these: "The greatest among you will be your servant," "The last will be first, and the first will be last," and "The one who is least among you all . . . is the greatest" (Matthew 23:11; Matthew 20:16; and Luke 9:48). You don't hear this kind of language very often in our world. It's usually about the most powerful, the best, or the smartest. But a humble servant's heart gives God great pleasure.

Christian singer Wayne Watson wrote a song called "Looking Out for Number One." He puts a clever spin on the popular phrase by saying, "Jesus is still in control of my life . . . So I guess you could say I'm looking out for number one."[2] If Jesus is your number one, then you have your priorities worked out well. Look out for Jesus, look out for others, and then look out for yourself. Just call yourself number three.

Daily Challenge

Think of several ways to serve other people today. Help someone with chores or homework or yard work. Choose to help someone who wouldn't expect it.

Devo 68

Eh? Meh? Bleh? Yeah!

Read Matthew 21:1–11; 14–17.

So, Ted," says Red, "What do you think of the beautiful Da Vinci painting *Mona Lisa*?"

"Eh," says Ted. "My five-year-old cousin could've drawn that."

"What do you think of Beethoven's Fifth Symphony?" asks Red.

"Meh. I've played better songs on my kazoo," says Ted.

"What about the Grand Canyon?" says Red.

"Bleh. I've got bigger holes in my jeans," says Ted.

Sometimes we're pretty picky about deciding what's worthy of our praise. It's so much easier to criticize.

The people in today's Scripture passage knew exactly who deserved their praise: Jesus.

It was Sunday when Jesus rode into Jerusalem on a donkey. (We celebrate this day on Palm Sunday, which is the Sunday before Easter.) This was the first day of the worst week in Jesus' life, but it started out okay. The people in Jerusalem recognized who He was and shouted at Him with the words, "Hosanna in the highest." They called Him Lord and proclaimed Him King. It must have made Jesus smile, at least for a moment. Even though He knew what was coming in just five days . . .

The chief priests and teachers were more like Ted. It seems like nothing Jesus did would ever impress them. All the healing, all the miracles, all the powerful, wise teachings, and still they said, "Eh. My grandma can feed twenty people with one pot roast. Feeding five thousand people with five loaves of bread and two fish isn't that big of a deal."

Loquacious Learning with Eugene

When the people were waving palm branches and laying them in front of Jesus as He entered the city of Jerusalem, they were observing a celebration also mentioned in Psalm 118. In the earlier observance, the people praised God for His saving acts and thanked Him for restoring and rescuing His broken and oppressed people from slavery in Egypt. At the time of Jesus' entry into Jerusalem, the Romans ruled over the people of Israel. The people desperately needed a Savior. Jesus was their Savior, though He rescued them in a much different way than He did in Egypt.[1]

Jesus has done so much to deserve your praise. He helps you. He heals you. He gives your life meaning. He loves you. He laid down His life for you. Worship Him like you believe all that!

Daily Challenge

Research *palm branches* in an encyclopedia or on the Internet (with your parents' permission) to see what they look like. Make a palm branch out of brown-and-green construction paper. Then reenact the scene when Jesus came into Jerusalem on a donkey. Sing praise songs to worship Him.

Devo 69

A Visit with the King

Read Matthew 21:12–13.

Nate and his mother won a contest and were invited to have dinner with the king at the palace. But Nate's mom forgot all about the dinner until the last minute.

"Just wear your jeans with the hole in the knee," she said, "and your football jersey."

Nate reminded her that they hadn't been washed since the chili war last Thursday.

"Don't worry about it. Wear them anyway," Mom said.

Nate and his mom arrived at the palace forty-five minutes late. When they walked through the door, Nate didn't even greet the king or bow. He scurried right past him to the royal living room, took off his shoes, turned on the television, and stretched out on the couch. Meanwhile, Nate's mother said to the king and queen, "I hope you don't mind. We got some burgers on the way here. We figured we wouldn't like the food you guys are serving."

Throughout dinner, Nate burped, and Nate's mother told a bunch of jokes she had heard about how dumb the king was. The king and queen looked at each other in dismay.

Can you imagine showing this kind of disrespect to someone in his or her house?

People today are increasingly disrespectful toward those in authority. They also disrespect the greatest authority—God. They often use God's name in disrespectful ways and ignore His commands. His Son, Jesus, is even portrayed in movies and books as goofy, powerless, or mean.

Wandering with Wooton

My mom always told me it was disrespectful to put my elbows on the table during dinner. I remember saying, "Mom! I'm twenty-eight years old, and I paid for this table! Why can't I put my elbows on it?" I guess it's just one of those manners things that I still don't get. Why is it disrespectful to hold down the table? But there are ways to show respect that I do understand . . . like thanking God for the food before meals, paying attention when the Bible is being taught, and not talking in church. Those are ways to respect God and show that we're excited to worship Him.

People were disrespectful in New Testament times too. When Jesus turned over the merchants' tables in the temple, He was angry that people were being disrespectful toward God and were dishonoring His temple. They were using the temple as a marketplace and were cheating the worshippers. The temple was the house of God. It was supposed to be used for prayer, not for making money.

Do we ever disrespect God or His house of worship? We may not burp or curse or wear dirty clothes to church, but do we say and do things that dishonor God? God is our friend and He loves us, but He is also the holy Creator of the universe. He is the King of Kings and deserves our respect. We can show God that we respect and love Him by worshipping Him, reading His Word, and obeying His commands. God loves it when we honor Him this way!

Daily Challenge

List five things you can do this week to show respect for God. What can you do at church? At school? At home? When you're playing outside? When you hear something on TV or from your friends that is disrespectful?

Devo 70

One Lazy Tree

Read Matthew 21:18–22.

And now it's time for . . . "Famous Quotes from Lazy People":

> "Four score and seven years ago . . . was pretty much the last time I got out of bed before noon." (Abraham Lazeon)
>
> "I have not yet begun to sit!" (John Paul Moans)
>
> "Ask what your country can do for you. Then ask a few more times." (Yawn F. Kennedy)

There aren't that many famous lazy people, are there? That's because lazy people don't accomplish much. The Bible has some harsh things to say about laziness. Proverbs 10:5 (NIRV) says, "A child who gathers crops in summer is wise. But a child who sleeps at harvest time brings shame."

Jesus had something to say about that in today's Scripture passage. Jesus wasn't actually angry at a fig tree. He was making a point about bearing fruit in our lives. If we don't bear fruit and faithfully follow God's commands, then we're worthless to the kingdom of God. God wants us to accomplish something with our lives by bearing fruit for Him!

Look around you . . . do you see laziness in yourself or your friends? Do you spend more time in front of the television, playing video games, and surfing the Internet than doing constructive things? Some constructive things you could do

Wandering with Wooton

Lazy days are okay every now and then. But with me, sometimes it gets out of hand. Like once, over summer break when I was in middle school, I suddenly realized it had been so long since I had changed out of my pajamas that I had grown out of them–while wearing them! I always feel better on days when I accomplish something.

include exercising, praying and reading your Bible, having meaningful conversations with your parents, and serving others.

Instead of being lazy, accomplish something! Be significant. Bear fruit. Serve God. Change the world.

And don't be like that famous lazy person Martin Loafer King Jr., who said, "All I do is dream . . ."

Never mind. I don't feel like finishing this quote.

Daily Challenge

Make a list of everything you want to accomplish the rest of this month—even things you know you probably won't get to. Set goals. How many tasks do you want to cross off your list? If you accomplish a goal, think of a reward for yourself. Get in the habit of getting stuff done!

Acrostic from Matthew

Answer the following questions and put them in grid horizontally. When you're done, a vertical word will appear in the shaded boxes–then you'll know how many people Jesus fed in one day (Matthew 14:21).

Questions:

1. In Matthew 19:21, Jesus told a rich young man, "If you want to be perfect, go, sell your possessions. . . . Then come ____ me." (Devo 65)
2. Famous painting by Leonardo Da Vinci. (Devo 68, two words)
3. In which Odyssey episode does Donna worry about her parents getting a divorce? (Devo 64, two words)
4. In Matthew 21:12-13, Jesus overturned the merchants' tables in the ____. (Devo 69)
5. "The last will be first, and the first will be ____." (Devo 67)
6. One thing that can't be separated: ____ milk. (Devo 64)
7. A famous selfish saying: "I'm looking out for number _____." (Devo 67)
8. The Sunday before Easter when Jesus rode into Jerusalem on a donkey. (Devo 68, two words)

Puzzle #10

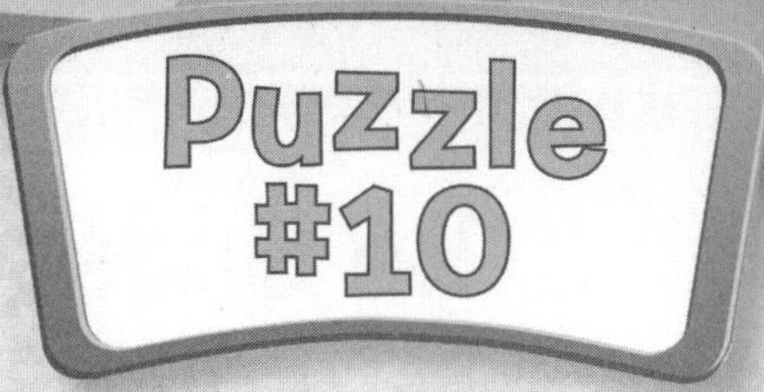

9. "The one who is least among you all . . . is the ____." (Devo 67)

10. Something Jesus made available to everyone, even criminals. (Devo 66)

11. What did Jesus tell Lenny to give to the poor? (Devo 65)

12. If we don't faithfully follow God's commands, then we're worthless to the____of God. (Devo 70)

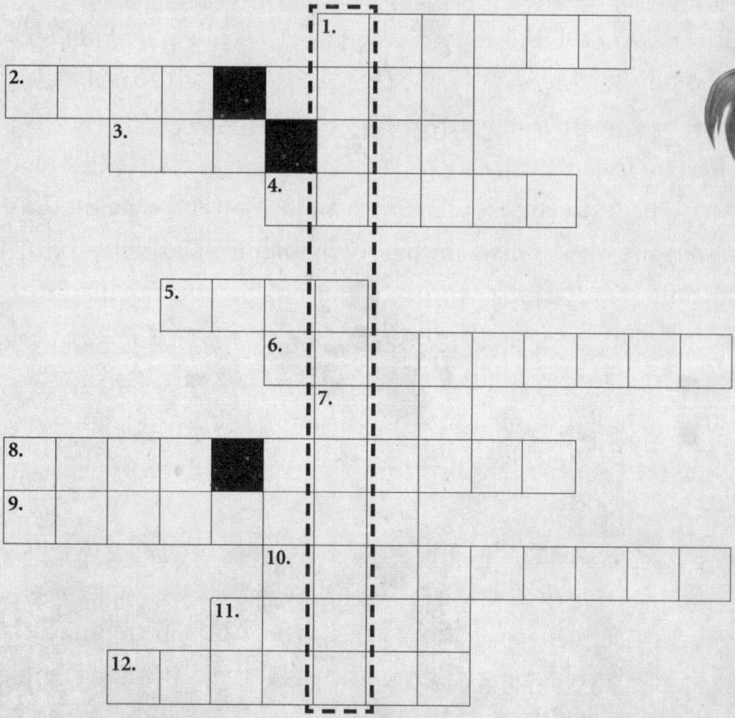

1.
2.
3.
4.
5.
6.
7.
8.
9.
10.
11.
12.

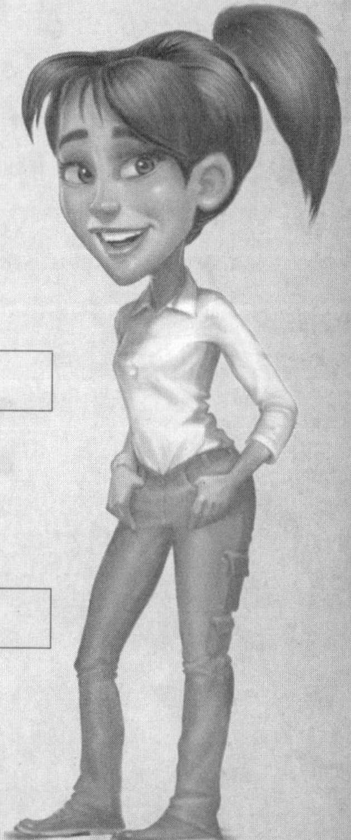

Answers on page 211.

Devo 71

The Guest List

Read Matthew 21:23–46; 22:1–14.

Jane put a sign on her bedroom door that read, "'GIRLS' CLUB. NO BOYS ALLOWED." Her younger brother, Jimmy, was mad because he wasn't invited to be in her club. So he went to his own room and put up a sign that read, "CHESS CLUB. CHESS PLAYERS ONLY." Jane was angry. She didn't know how to play chess. So she put a sign on her door that read, "AUGUST BIRTHDAY CLUB. AUGUST BIRTHDAYS ONLY." Jimmy was mad. His birthday was in June. So he put a sign on his door that read, "BLUE EYES CLUB." You can probably guess what color Jane's eyes *weren't*.

Have you ever felt bad because you weren't invited to some special event? Or have you ever wanted so badly to be part of a club but didn't meet the conditions? God doesn't exclude anyone who wants to be part of His family. The invitation is open to all through faith in Jesus Christ. Anyone who trusts in Jesus can inherit the kingdom of God.

In today's Bible reading, Jesus told three parables about entering His kingdom. The first parable is about two sons, one who repented of his sin and one who didn't. The point of the parable is that anyone who *repents* can enter the kingdom of God.

The second parable is about tenants who rented some land from a landowner. When the landowner's son came to visit them, they rejected and killed him. Jesus was talking here about people who reject Him as God's Son. God's kingdom will be taken away from those who reject Jesus. But those who *believe* in Him will be welcomed into His kingdom.

Whit's Wisdom

The Pharisees weren't too happy about any of these parables. All three were about them, and none of them were very complimentary. They were like the son who didn't repent. They were like the ones who rejected and killed the landowner's son. They were like the ones who ignored the king's wedding invitation. Stories like these angered the Pharisees so much that they eventually nailed Jesus to a cross. Some people have a hard time with the truth.

The third story is about a king who sent out an invitation for a wedding party at the palace. Many ignored the invitation and were taken off the guest list. But others accepted the invitation and were welcomed to the feast. The lesson of this parable is like the others: People who *accept* God's invitation to join His family will be part of the kingdom of God.

Repent. Believe. Accept. These are the steps for making sure you're on God's guest list and part of His family forever.

Daily Challenge

Write your own parable. First, think of a message you want to communicate in a creative way, such as honesty, Jesus' love, patience, or the importance of prayer. Next, come up with characters that represent the people or ideas in your story. For example, a bad king could represent the devil. Third, come up with a story that illustrates your message. Write down the story and draw pictures to go along with it.

Devo 72

The Best Teammate

Read Matthew 22:15–33; 41–46.

Lev Yashin of the USSR was arguably the greatest soccer goalie in history. In the 1950s, he was called the "Black Spider" because he seemed to have eight arms and legs to block shots. In 812 career games, he had almost 500 shutouts (called "clean sheets), which means he allowed zero goals in the entire match.[1]

If you had the ball and were approaching the goal, you had Yashin to deal with. Chances are, you weren't getting the ball past him. What a great teammate to have! You'd feel confident knowing you had someone like that to stop the other team from scoring.

In today's Scripture passage, Jesus was the Lev Yashin of trick questions. Everything the Pharisees kicked at Him, He kicked right back. The Pharisees would smile evil smiles as they approached Jesus with what they thought was an impossible question for Him to answer. Every time, they left humiliated, with a confused look on their faces and their tails between their legs. Jesus watched them come back again and again, and it was as if He was saying, "Hit me with your best shot."

Jesus answered tricky questions about taxes, marriage, and the resurrection of souls. And when the Pharisees finally finished quizzing him, we find one of the funniest verses in the entire Bible: "From that day on, no one dared to ask him any more questions" (Matthew 22:46). Guess not. Who would want to endure another humiliating defeat?

Indeed, Jesus makes a great teammate. What a wise resource to have in your corner. If you're confused, go to Jesus. He has the answers. If you're having

Loquacious Learning with Eugene

Once I was on a team for an academic competition called Brainiacs. It was on local-access television, and the moderator asked obvious questions, such as "How many lanthanides are radioactive?" To borrow the rough colloquialism, "Duh! It's one!"[2] I learned that in elementary school! My teammates called me the "man with all the answers." But when I began my employment at Whit's End, I discovered that when it came to matters of faith, I didn't have many answers at all! Since becoming a Christian, I try to refer to the words of Jesus to help me with important questions of life.

trouble believing something, go to Jesus. He will erase your doubts. If you have a moral problem and don't know how to deal with it, go to Jesus. He will give you direction.

There's a reason why Ephesians 6:17 calls the Word of God your "sword." It's a fantastic weapon against an enemy who wants to confuse you. Say to the devil, "Hit me with your best shot." You have the perfect goalie on your side.

Daily Challenge

Think of some hard questions you've had in the past about the world, the Bible, or God. Research the Bible to find answers for your questions. Also talk about your questions with your parents or a Sunday school teacher.

Devo 73

Bible Law Cheat Sheet

Read Matthew 22:34–40.

"Teacher, which is the greatest commandment in the Law?" the Pharisees asked Jesus (Matthew 22:36).

This wasn't a new question. Other rabbis had been asked this question before. Maybe it was hard to keep track of all the laws because there were so many of them.

Other teachers had answered, "Don't do anything to someone that you wouldn't want someone to do to you." So don't hit someone if you don't want to be hit. Don't steal from someone if you don't want to be stolen from. But Jesus took this a step further when He said, "Love others as you love yourself." Treat others the way you want to be treated. Don't just avoid hurting others. Go out of your way to care for them.

That's command number two. The first and greatest command Jesus named was, "Love the Lord your God with all your heart and with all your soul and with all your mind" (verse 37). With these rules, you can pretty much determine what to do in any situation. Ask yourself, "By doing or saying this, am I loving God? By doing or saying this, am I loving others?"

If you can answer yes to both questions, you're probably making a good choice. But if you know you'll be disobeying God or hurting others, then you need to rethink your choice.

God's ways aren't meant to be complicated. He's not trying to load you down with tons of rules and requirements. But He does know the best way for you to live—by loving Him and loving others.

Wandering with Wooton

As a mailman, I come across some really nice people on my route—and some less than nice ones. Like Mrs. Kramer, who always grumbles about my being late or accuses me of stealing her packages. (I always tell her that I don't need a new wig. I've got plenty!) But instead of getting mad back, I decided to be extra nice to her. I tried to think of the things I like. I like milkshakes, so I brought her one. I like when people say nice things to me, so I complimented her on her glasses. I like it when people help me out, so I asked if I could walk her poodle for her. Even though I haven't seen much change in her attitude, treating Mrs. Kramer with love made life better for both of us (and her poodle!).

Daily Challenge

Write in your school notebook: "Am I loving God? Am I loving others?" Get in the habit of asking yourself these questions throughout the day.

Devo 74

Woe, Woe, Woe!

Read Matthew 23:1–39.

The beautiful four-foot-tall wedding cake stood in the center of the banquet hall. Guests surrounded it, gushing over how magnificent it was, with hundreds of handcrafted sugar flowers and perfectly frosted peaks. A cascade of roses flowed down one side.

The happy bride and groom made their way to cut the first piece. Slicing gently into the soft, creamy pastry, they handed each other a bite to try. But their smiles of anticipation quickly changed to disgusted grimaces as they gagged and spit out the cake. The mystery was soon solved: The baker had accidentally made the cake with a package of salt instead of a package of sugar!

We've all been fooled by attractive-looking exteriors. A book cover might look interesting, but the story inside is dull. New jeans look great in the store, but they start falling apart once you get them home. The girl behind you in English class seems nice and fun. But the more you talk to her, you realize she gossips a lot and really doesn't have anything nice to say about anyone.

The Pharisees looked good on the outside too. They seemed to follow God perfectly—almost too perfectly. For example, the "phylacteries" mentioned in Matthew 23:5 were small boxes with Scripture tucked inside. Jewish men would tie the boxes around their arms as a symbol of keeping God's Word close to their hearts. But the Pharisees made their boxes "wide" so people would notice them and be impressed by their holiness.

Instead of using phylacteries as reminder to honor God, the Pharisees were using them to gain recognition and honor. That's not what God intended!

Loquacious Learning with Eugene

The tassels mentioned in Matthew 23:5 were tied to the hems of men's robes. They were meant as a reminder to the Jews to follow God's commands rather than their own desires (see Numbers 15:37-41). Though the Pharisees were following the letter of the law, they were missing its intent. They made their tassels long and obvious, using them to draw attention to themselves instead of God.

In today's Scripture passage, Jesus is telling us to be more concerned about what God thinks of our thoughts and behavior than making ourselves look good.

Daily Challenge

You probably aren't tying big boxes of Scripture around your arm, but take an honest look at your life. Have you "dressed up" the outside of your life but neglected to clean the hidden parts of your heart? Do you act a certain way at church and a different way at school? Do you harbor anger or envy in your heart? God wants us to clean the inside of our lives first and not worry about what others think of the outside.

Devo 75

There's Comin' a Day . . .

Read Matthew 24:1-35.

Okay, kids," said the father to his family. "This is going to be our vacation this year. On Monday we're going to pile all eight of you into a small car with no working windows for a fourteen-hour drive through the desert. On Tuesday we're going to lie on a frozen tundra in our pajamas. On Wednesday we're entering an asparagus-sardine-cough-medicine-eating contest. On Thursday we're going swimming with the piranhas! On Friday we're going to have our wisdom teeth taken out by hyperactive preschoolers with pliers. On Saturday we'll visit an amusement park we've rented out just for our family. Then we'll take a helicopter ride, eat unlimited ice cream all day, and have dinner on a yacht with the president of the United States, the Super Bowl MVP, and all your favorite movie actors."

The rest of the week almost seems worth it when you think about Saturday's lineup, huh?

In today's Scripture reading, Jesus had some tough news for His disciples about what was coming. He talked about wars, earthquakes, destruction, false teachers, starvation, death, hatred, and suffering. The sun would be darkened; the moon would stop shining. Depressing stuff. But . . . a better day is coming! A better day is coming! Jesus will appear in the sky with power and great glory. The trumpets will sound, and all of His chosen people will celebrate the coming of the new King. Jesus will take us with Him back to heaven, where there will be no more pain or suffering.

There are lots of depressing things in our world right now—disease, natural

Whit's Wisdom

The Bible has a lot to say about the last days before Jesus returns. There are many prophecies in the books of Daniel, Ezekiel, Zechariah, and Revelation. Jesus Himself spoke about His return on a number of occasions. It may seem scary, but Jesus gives us hope when He said in Matthew 24:35, "Heaven and earth will pass away, but my words will never pass away." The world may fall apart around us, but Jesus is here to stay.

disasters, orphans, wars, poverty, and more. In the last days before Jesus comes back, it's going to get worse. But then it will get better—*much* better.

Whenever you get discouraged, remember Jesus' promise that He will come again. As long as we're followers of Jesus, we have hope for the future. There will be a happy ending for believers because Jesus has promised that we'll spend eternity with Him.

As we wait for His return, Jesus gives us hope and encouragement in the middle of sadness. He fills us with peace even when everything around us is falling apart. And when all seems lost, He reminds us that we have an incredible future in store with Him. It's going to be a great day!

Daily Challenge

Draw a picture, write a story or poem, or simply imagine what that day will be like when Jesus returns to the earth. What do you think you'll do when you see Him?

Devo 76

Get Ready!

Read Matthew 24:36–51; 25:1–13.

Pope Sylvester II and others predicted Jesus would return to earth on January 1, 1000, a thousand years after His birth.[1] Mathematician Michael Stifel used his math skills to predict Jesus' return on October 19, 1533 at 8:00 a.m.[2] (Maybe Mr. Stifel should have used a calculator—so far his prediction was about five hundred years off.)

Cotton Mather, a Puritan minister, predicted the end of the world in 1697. It didn't happen, so he switched it to 1716. Didn't happen again, so he decided it was 1736.[3] Nuts! Wrong again!

George Rapp, founder of the Harmony Society, predicted that Jesus was coming back sometime during his lifetime. Even on his deathbed, he told his friends that Jesus would come.[4] It was if he was saying, "Okay, He's coming . . . now! No . . . now! Okay, wait for it . . . now!"

There are lots of people throughout history with prophetic egg on their faces. If they had only read today's Scripture passage, they would have figured out that no amount of calculations, wisdom, or educated guesses would help them predict when Jesus is going to return. Jesus made it very clear that no one on earth knows the day or time—or will ever know until it actually happens. Not even the angels in heaven know. Even Jesus Himself didn't know!

In the *Odyssey* episode "The Second Coming" (album 10), Melanie Jacobs reads a book by a man who claimed he knew the very day when Jesus would return—and it was Saturday! She gets so excited, she puts up posters all over town. On the big night, she sets up a tent in her backyard and watches the skies closely.

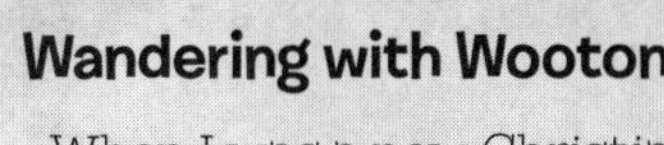

Wandering with Wooton

When I was a new Christian, I saw this guy on TV predict the end of the world. I freaked out. It was really scary. I bought up all of the licorice I could find, stored it in vacuum-sealed jars, and placed it in an underground bomb shelter. Bottled water and canned vegetables would have been a good idea too, but you know, I was in panic mode and only worried about the necessities. Now I'm not worried about the end of the world anymore. To get ready for Jesus coming back, I want to tell everyone I know about Him. I don't want anyone left behind.

Jesus doesn't come, but that doesn't dampen Melanie's enthusiasm about Jesus' return.

Jesus told us to be ready for His return. He even told a parable about people who were ready and people who weren't. How do we get ready? Do we pitch a tent and stare into the skies? No. We prepare our hearts. If you've never made a decision to make Jesus the Lord of your life, don't wait. You don't want to be one of the people on the outside looking in.

In the meantime, focus on becoming more like Jesus before He does return.

Daily Challenge

Think about what you want to be doing when Jesus returns. Discuss it with family or friends. It may change the way you use your time when you know that He could show up at any moment.

Devo 77

Talents and Troubles

Read Matthew 25:14–30.

In the parable of the talents, Jesus told about a master who left on a trip and gave each of his servants some money (or talents) to be responsible for. The talents represent the things God has given each of us. It could mean finances, abilities, gifts, wisdom, relationships, opportunities, or even a sense of humor!

In the story, two of the servants successfully invested the talents the master entrusted them with, increasing his wealth. The third servant, however, was afraid to risk investing the talents, so he decided to bury them instead.

This is like Jared DeWhite in the *Odyssey* episode "The Buck Starts Here" (album 33). Whit challenges three kids from Whit's End with a similar test. With twenty-five dollars in hand, Nathaniel and Ashley each start a business. But Jared, fearful that someone is trying to get his money, buries it in the park instead.

A key verse in Jesus' parable is the third servant's response when the master returned: "I knew that you are a hard man. . . . So I was afraid and went out and hid your talent in the ground" (Matthew 25:24–25). He was *afraid* of the master and made his decision out of fear of what the master would do if he tried and failed.

Because of this, the master *did* respond angrily. But it wasn't about the money. (After all, this story is about God, who already owns everything anyway.) The master was angry that the servant didn't use what he had. The master was also angry that the servant acted out of fear instead of trying to do his best on his master's behalf.

God has created us each uniquely with specific "talents." Every gift He has given us is for a purpose. But we're sometimes afraid to use our talents because

Wandering with Wooton

When I was growing up, I didn't think I had a whole lot of gifts or talents. I mean, I could balance a stack of seventeen pennies on my nose while gargling the "Hallelujah Chorus". But I always ran the wrong way in baseball, and dogs always started howling when I was singing. But one day while I was doing my penny-and-gargling trick, I noticed a whole bunch of people watching me. And I realized the gift God gave me is that I really like people. I like being around them, hearing their stories, telling them about my life, and making them laugh. My gift is people! I never realized it was a gift before, but now I see that God made me that way for a reason!

we don't want to look foolish or fail. Jesus is saying, "It's okay if you fail—just step out and take a risk."

The gifts God gives are limitless. But how much we use them is up to us.

Daily Challenge

List the gifts you think God gave you. Maybe you have a great singing voice, a knack for leading people, or a special passion for prayer. You can even ask your parents and friends to weigh in on what they see as your gifts and talents. Commit to using each of the gifts and talents on your list to serve God.

Math Code

When the Pharisees were trying to lure Jesus into a verbal trap (Matthew 22:15-22), they asked Him if it was right to pay taxes. Using the number key, decode the message below to see Jesus' reply.

1 = God's

2 = to

3 = give

4 = Caesar

5 = God

6 = what

7 = and

8 = is

9 = Caesar's

Puzzle #11

______ 17 - 14	______ 10 ÷ 5	______ 20 - 16
______ 24 ÷ 4	______ 2 x 4	______ 32 - 23
______ 21 ÷ 3	______ 8 - 6	______ 1 + 4
______ 11 - 5	______ 5 + 3	______ 1 x 1

Answer on page 211.

Devo 78

The Shoemaker

Read Matthew 25:31–46.

Leo Tolstoy wrote a short story called "Where Love Is, God Is."[1] The story is about a shoemaker named Martin. His shop is in a basement, and through one window, he can see the feet of everyone walking by on the street. One night he has two dreams where he hears a voice saying, "Martin! Look tomorrow on the street! I am coming!" Martin believes it was Jesus telling him He was coming.

So the next day, he looks out the window at the feet going by, waiting to see the shoes of Jesus. Instead, he sees an old man named Stepanich, who runs a shop next door. Stepanich tries to shovel the snow from the sidewalk, but he is frail and cold. Martin brews him a pot of tea and invites him inside. Stepanich stays a while and then goes on his way.

Martin looks out the window for Jesus again. A woman with her baby comes by. The baby cries from the cold. Martin invites them in, feeds them, and gives the woman his coat to keep them warm. The woman expresses her thanks and leaves.

Martin goes back to his window. Still he doesn't see Jesus. But he does see a woman tussling with a young boy who has just stolen one of her apples. Martin goes out and makes peace between them. Then he pays the woman for the apple so that the apologetic boy can keep it. The woman and the boy go on their way.

Nighttime comes, and Martin is disappointed he hasn't seen Jesus. But then he hears voices coming from the corner of the room. "Martin. Do you recognize me?"

Martin said, "Who?"

Connie's Corner

The story of the sheep and the goats in Matthew 25 always gets me thinking. I remember all the times I ignored or forgot about people who needed help, but this story makes me realize that I might as well have ignored God Himself. Ouch! Whit once gave me a stuffed sheep as a Christmas present. I didn't know what it meant at first, but then I figured it out. Be a sheep, not a goat.

One by one, Stepanich, the mother, the apple seller, and the thief step out, saying, "It is I." All of them smile and then vanish.

Martin reaches for his Bible and reads, "I was hungry and you gave me something to eat. I was thirsty and you gave me something to drink. I was a stranger and you invited me in. . . . Whatever you did for one of the least [important] of these brothers of mine, you did for me" (Matthew 25:35, 40).*

Serve others, and you serve God.

Daily Challenge

Who are the "least important of these" in your life? Make a list of people you might ignore or not think about very often. How can you serve them as if they were Jesus?

* You can listen to a retelling of Tolstoy's story in the *Odyssey* episode "B-TV: Compassion" (album 27).

Devo 79

Good Versus Better

Read Matthew 26:1–13.

Choose one from each pair of options: Cookies or ice cream? Swimming or skating? Zoo or water park?

Tough choices! You have to decide between two really good things. So did the woman in today's Scripture passage. She walked into Simon's house, saw Jesus, broke open an expensive bottle of perfume, and began pouring it over Jesus' head.

The disciples complained, "She could've sold that perfume for a lot of money and given it to the poor!"

It's a solid argument, actually. Jesus tells us to give to the poor. So the woman had to decide between two very good things—helping the poor or showing affection for Jesus.

So how do you decide between good and better things?

Think about this scenario: You walk into church, heading to the auditorium, and you find out that one of the childcare workers called in sick. You really wanted to go to the worship service, but the children's church really needs help with the littler kids. The Bible says to serve others, but it also tells us to worship God. Both of those things are good. How do you choose?

There's really no easy answer. In today's passage, Jesus told His disciples that He was only on Earth for a short time. The poor would be there long after He was gone. In this case, the woman chose correctly. She chose to honor God and His Son, Jesus.

When your motivation is to give God your best, it's hard to go wrong. Also, when you honor God, He will honor you. Jesus praised the woman in front of

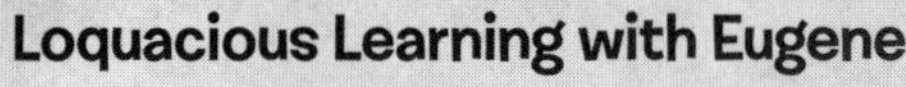

Loquacious Learning with Eugene

The perfume the woman poured onto Jesus' head was called nard, a fragrant ointment used after a person has died. We know that the perfume was nard from an account of the same event in John 12. The woman isn't identified here, but we know from John 12 that she was Mary, the sister of Lazarus. Since the perfume is often used to prepare a body for burial, Mary may have guessed that Jesus was going to die. She may have felt she wouldn't get the chance again to honor the Man who raised her brother from the dead (John 11).

everyone, saying, "What she has done will be told anywhere this good news is preached all over the world. It will be told in memory of her" (Matthew 26:13, NIrV).

How do we honor Jesus? By taking time to worship Him, spending time with Him in prayer and Bible reading, and doing the things He commanded us to do. Do these things, and you'll stay on the path He wants you on.

Daily Challenge

Think of some new ways to show God how much you love Him. It may involve music, writing, drawing, speaking to a group of people, hosting a get-together at your house, or something else. Be creative!

Devo 80

Dinner with Friends

Read Matthew 26:14–25; 31–35.

If you had only one more day to live, whom would you want to spend your last meal with? A stranger? Your math teacher? The guy down the street whose house smells like onions? The president of the United States? Or would you want to spend that time with the people who have meant the most in your life?

Jesus chose to eat His last meal with His best friends—the disciples. It was Thursday night. Jesus knew He would be dead at that time the very next day. But He had one final night with these twelve men who meant so much to Him. He would spend it teaching a final lesson.

The disciples prepared a room and cooked some food. Then they joined Jesus at the table for the meal. Jesus pointed out that two of them were going to turn their backs on Him: Judas would betray Him, and Peter would deny knowing Him. Sure enough, both of those things happened later that night.

Jesus knew all of this, and yet He still wanted to hang out with His friends. He spent the final hours of His life teaching them and sharing one last meal with them before things got messy.

As it turns out, Jesus had big plans for His disciples later on. Peter, after denying Jesus, would be put in charge of the Christian church after Jesus went back to heaven. The others would help to spread the good news about Jesus and build up the church. Peter and the other disciples would do a great job (except for Judas, of course).

What final lesson did Jesus teach that night? He knows that we will fail Him and sin against God more often than we'd want to admit. We may even pretend

Whit's Wisdom

The Bible is full of people God used in spite of their sin. Abraham was a liar, but God made him the "father of many nations" (Genesis 17:5). Moses was a murderer, but God used him to lead the Hebrew people out of Egypt (Exodus 3-4; 12:31-42). King David was an adulterer *and* a murderer, and yet God said he was "a man after my own heart" (Acts 13:22). God knows that we all fail sometimes. But He still loves us and has great plans for us.

we don't know Jesus. But Jesus still loves us. He still wants to hang out with us. And someday He may even use us to do amazing things in the world.

Daily Challenge

Read Peter's speech in Acts 2:14–41. Can you believe these powerful words came from the same man who, a short time before, cowered in fear and denied that Jesus was even his friend? If God could use Peter this way after a big failure, don't you think He can use you even when you fail? Why or why not?

Devo 81

Remember

Read Matthew 26:26–30.

Jackson brought a shell home from vacation so he'd remember his time on the beach.

Julia pinned a picture of her best friend on her bulletin board so she'd always remember her after she moved away.

Grant always quotes a favorite movie line to his friends on the basketball team. It makes them laugh and remember the fun they had watching the movie together.

Mom keeps a photo album with pictures of every Christmas and Easter.

Savannah keeps a trophy on her bedside table that she won in the equestrian competition.

It's important to remember special events in our lives. God made us this way!

When God parted the Jordan River so the Israelites could cross it, He had them build a memorial of twelve large stones so they would remember that place (Joshua 4:1–7). Then when their children or grandchildren saw it and said, "Hey, Grandpa . . .," the Israelites could tell the story of how God provided for them.

Another way of remembering was through festivals. When God delivered the Israelites out of Egypt, they put blood on their doorposts so that the angel of death would "pass over" them and they'd be protected. Every year since that time, the Jewish people celebrate the festival of Passover to remember God's protection and guidance (Exodus 11–12).

Before He died, Jesus gave His disciples one more important memory: He celebrated the Passover with them. As they drank the wine and ate the bread, Jesus

Wandering with Wooton

I was taking Communion at church one Sunday, and I thought I heard the fire alarm go off. I jumped up and spilled a dozen little cups of grape juice on my new white shirt. I was really bummed about it. So were the other people in the pew who could only take half a Communion that week. But then I started to kind of like that shirt. The Bible says that Jesus' blood covers all our sins, and my stained shirt reminds me that I'm completely covered by God's forgiveness. So now it's one of my favorites! The fire alarm turned out to be my cell phone. I guess I can be a little jumpy.

told them about His death. In mere hours, His body would be broken, and His blood would be shed on the cross. For the rest of their lives, His disciples needed to remember Jesus' death and what it meant. We *all* need to remember.

We celebrate Communion because it reminds us of the greatest event in the history of the world. We remember the sacrifice Jesus made to pay for our sins. We think about the pain He suffered on the cross in our place. We receive the full forgiveness He offers. We celebrate because He gave His life so that everyone who trusts in Him can be saved. And because He was raised from the dead, we look forward to a future celebration with Him in heaven.

Now that's something worth remembering!

Daily Challenge

This week, suggest having Communion together as a family. You don't need to have fancy cups or special bread—you can even use pretzels and soda pop! The point is to remember together what Jesus did for each of you. Read through Matthew 26:26–30 together, and then pray, thanking Jesus for giving His life so you could go to heaven.

Devo 82

Thy Will Be Done

Read Matthew 26:36-46.

Joni Eareckson Tada was only a teenager when a diving accident left her paralyzed. She woke to find herself in a hospital bed, unable to use her arms or legs. At that moment she knew that her life would never be the same. For years she would pray fervently for God to heal her. She knew He could. But that healing never happened, and she remained confined to a wheelchair.

Today Joni can honestly say she's glad that God didn't say yes to those prayers from her hospital bed. In one interview she said, "The 'no' answer to a prayer for healing has meant a more urgent leaning upon Him every day, a more vibrant hope of heaven, a deeper sense of prayer, a more energetic love for His Word. It's fostered my friendships, and deepened my concern and compassion for others who hurt. It's helped me start [a] ministry."[1]

Despite being disabled, Joni has allowed God to use her in amazing ways. She's learned to paint beautiful paintings using a pen in her mouth. She's written many books that help people in their walk with the Lord. And she's started a ministry to help other people who are struggling with disabilities. God has been glorified in Joni's life. People have come to know Him through her, and Joni herself has been transformed through her tragedy.[2]

In today's Scripture passage, we find Jesus praying in the garden of Gethsemane. In just a few hours, He will face death. He knows what He's in for. It's why He came to Earth as a human in the first place: to become the ultimate Sacrifice and save us from our sins.

But now His time has come, and torture is only hours away. He is deeply trou-

Connie's Corner

It was very hard when my grandma died. I loved her so much, and it was hard for me to believe that losing her was God's will. But through her death, my mom came to Christ, which was amazing! I see now how God used a sad situation for good, and it helps me remember that His plans are always wiser than ours.

bled and "overwhelmed with sorrow to the point of death" (Matthew 26:38). The end is coming, and it will be anything but easy.

As Jesus prays, He pleads with His Father, "If there be any other way . . ." Yet even though Jesus wanted God to provide a way out, He trusted His Father and said, "Your will be done" (verse 42).

We don't always understand why bad things happen. But like Jesus and Joni, we can trust God's plan for us. He can use anything for His glory and our good. Because He knows what's best for us, He can work things out in ways we could never imagine. Best of all, He promises He will always be with us in our struggles. He'll never leave us alone.

Daily Challenge

Journal about a difficult time you've gone through. How did God help you through that time? What did you learn from it?

Devo 83

The Ultimate Puzzle Maker

Read Matthew 26:47–56.

What if someone gave you a piece to a puzzle you've never seen? That piece might contain something green with an edge of black. Is it an iguana? A bean? A rotting pickle? You don't know because you can't see the whole puzzle.

It's a lot like your life. You can only see one small part of the puzzle, and that piece doesn't always make sense. *But God created puzzles*. He knows how everything fits together because He designed it that way.

When you finally realize that the puzzle piece someone gave you fits into a puzzle of a beautiful waterfall in Ecuador, you understand the importance of each piece. Without every piece, the puzzle wouldn't be complete.

In today's Scripture passage, the strangest piece of the resurrection puzzle is Judas's betrayal. Judas was one of the twelve disciples. He had lived with Jesus, walked with Him for thousands of miles, eaten with Him, laughed with Him. How could one of Jesus' closest friends betray Him?

Jesus knew why, because He's the Master Puzzle Maker. In fact, Jesus had told Judas, "What you are about to do, do quickly" (John 13:27). Jesus already knew what was going to happen. It was all part of His Father's plan.

You see, nothing surprises God. Nothing causes Him to scramble and try to rework the pieces of His puzzle. He knows what He's doing—and He's always known.

Without Judas's betrayal, the whole salvation story wouldn't have come together as God intended.

Proverbs 16:9 says, "In his heart a man plans his course, but the Lord deter-

Loquacious Learning with Eugene

In the first century, Judas was actually a very popular name. In fact, the New Testament mentions at least four people named Judas. Judas Iscariot betrayed Jesus. Judas the Zealot was another disciple of Jesus. Judas the Galilean, who is mentioned in Acts 5, led a violent revolt. And the apostle Saul visited a man named Judas when he was blinded on the road to Damascus. But when Judas betrayed Christ, the name became very unpopular. Even today that name isn't listed in the top thousand names for new babies.

mines his steps." God knows each puzzle piece in your life, each part of your story. And when all the pieces are finally connected, you'll see the beautiful picture He had in mind all along.

Daily Challenge

Think of your life as a puzzle. What part of your life doesn't make sense right now because you can't see the whole picture? How do you know that God will work things out?

Devo 84

Lose a Battle, Win a War

Read Matthew 26:57–68.

His trainers prayed before the fight that he wouldn't get killed. Everyone was expecting the other guy to win. And for seven rounds of the world heavyweight boxing championship, Muhammad Ali made it look as if they were going to be right.

The boxing match was in Zaire, Africa, on October 30, 1974. (Zaire is now the Republic of the Congo.) The fight was called the "Rumble in the Jungle." It was one of the most important boxing matches in history, between Muhammad Ali and George Foreman. In the first round of the fight, things were about even between them. But in the second round, Ali began to do something strange. He backed up against the outside ropes and let Foreman hit him. He punched back only sparingly, simply protecting his head with his arms. Foreman punched him repeatedly, but didn't hurt Ali at all. Ali did this for six more rounds. He just let Foreman swing away and feel as if he was winning.

By the eighth round, Foreman had spent so much energy that when Ali came back with a flurry of punches, Foreman stumbled and fell to the mat. He was down for the count, and Ali won. Ali was praised for using this "rope-a-dope" technique, where you allow your opponent to win a few battles before he loses the ultimate war.[1]

In today's Scripture passage, Jesus stood before Caiaphas, the high priest, for questioning. The religious leaders had falsely accused Jesus of all sorts of things, but He didn't put up a fight.

Jesus could have won the dispute with Caiaphas the high priest. Jesus had

Whit's Wisdom

When you're young, it's hard to consider the big picture. But God has been around since the beginning of time and will be until the end of it. His plans may not be our plans. We all need to learn to trust that His ultimate plans are better for us than our short-term ones.

calmed storms. He had raised people from the dead. He had fed thousands of people with five loaves of bread and two small fish.

When He was questioned by the high priest, Jesus could've gone all "Batman" on the guy and flattened him in a millisecond. Instead, Jesus was silent. He allowed the high priest to ask Him humiliating questions. He allowed people to spit on Him and hit Him. Why? Because Jesus knew He had a bigger war to fight and win. He was up against Satan, not Caiaphas and the Jewish leaders. God's ultimate plan was for Jesus to face down evil, die for the sins of the world, and rise again.

Whenever you find yourself struggling, remember the bigger picture. You might lose some battles along the way, but God has put you on this earth to serve Him and fulfill His ultimate plan for the world.

Daily Challenge

Think about your goals in life. What do you want to accomplish by the time you die? What do you think God wants to accomplish through you? Write it down. Obviously your personal goals are going to change over time, but God has an ultimate plan for the world that includes you! Whenever you set goals, always take time to think about God's ultimate plan and how your plans can fit into His. He has great things in store for you!

Hexagon Help

Put the words inside the hexagons in order by matching the symbols on the sides and creating a sentence that makes sense. You'll have to copy the word *and* the symbols into the blank hexagons. The first word is "Whatever," and we've filled in the next two words. (Hint: When you're done, you'll finish Matthew 25:40.)

"Whatever

■ ✷ ● you ✔ ▲ ✖

✖ ▲ ✔ did ● ✷ ■

Puzzle #12

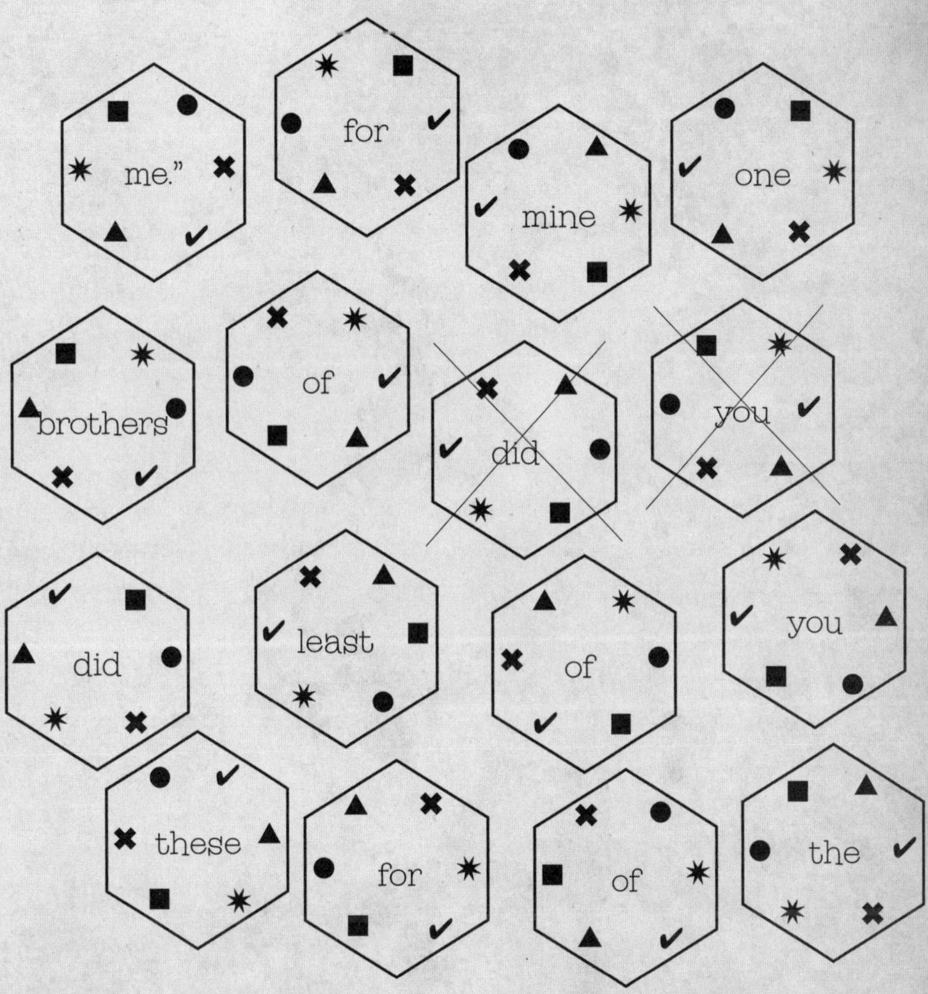

Answers on page 211.

Devo 85

Standing Up

Read Matthew 26:69–75.

In the *Odyssey* episode "Choices" (album 4), Lucy is given the best assignment she has ever had—to write a story for the *Educator*, a newspaper for district teachers. Then she learns that the assignment is to write about evolution. Lucy doesn't believe in the theory of evolution. She believes that the Bible tells the story of how God created humankind, not some theory about monkeys becoming human. She asks for another assignment, but her science teacher won't budge and refuses to change the topic. Either Lucy writes this paper, or she receives a failing grade.

Lucy doesn't know what to do, so she goes to Whit for advice. Whit tells her that if she believes in her heart that something is wrong, she shouldn't do it. He points to a Bible verse, Romans 14:23: "Everything that does not come from faith is sin."

Nervous, Lucy goes back to her teacher and tells him that she cannot do the assignment because she doesn't believe it would be right. She'll accept the failing grade. The teacher is so impressed by her conviction, he offers to change the assignment—a report on evolution from a Christian's perspective.

Sometimes it's hard to stand up for what you believe because others don't always understand your motives. If your friends are doing something wrong, it's hard to say no because they may make fun of you. It's hard to go against the crowd.

But think about how much harder it was for Peter when he *didn't* stand up for what he believed when Jesus was being arrested. He was probably afraid of being arrested too. So Peter played it safe. He denied that he even knew Jesus. And just

Connie's Corner

Once I went to a slumber party with some friends from school. One of them played a DVD called *The Bad Girls of Striped Alder Grove*. I could pretty much tell from the title that it had some inappropriate things in it, but I didn't say anything. I watched every last agonizingly awful minute of that movie. Ugh! Are there any responsible parents living in Striped Alder Grove? I felt so dirty and guilty the next day. The next time that girl asked me to come over, I politely said no. I wish I would've had the courage to say no the first time.

as Jesus predicted, the rooster crowed. After Peter realized what he had done, "he went outside and wept bitterly" (Matthew 26:75) Thinking he had disappointed Jesus was a far worse punishment than he would've gotten even if he had been thrown into jail.

Next time you're tempted to play it safe and go with the crowd, stand up for what you believe! God is pleased whenever we stand up for Him and His Word, even if it means being rejected or getting a failing grade in class!

Daily Challenge

Sometimes it helps to say aloud what your beliefs are. Pick one or two convictions and complete these statements aloud: "I will never _____ " or "I will always _____ ."Ask God to help you stick to your convictions.

Devo 86

A Guilty Conscience

Read Matthew 27:1–10.

Shakespeare's play *Macbeth* is the story of a man who wants to become king. There's one problem: King Duncan already rules the land. Macbeth tells his wife about his wish, and she plots with him to get rid of King Duncan. Their scheme works just as they hoped it would, and Macbeth becomes king.

That's when the trouble starts. Macbeth is racked with guilt. He can't sleep and sees haunting visions. His wife, Lady Macbeth, begins sleepwalking and having horrible nightmares. Eventually she loses her mind and dies of guilt. Macbeth is so sad after her death that he plans to die in battle against the rightful heir to the throne. In the last scene, he struggles with his guilt and admits to killing the king.[1]

Guilt is also what killed Judas Iscariot. In today's Scripture passage, we see that he felt so bad for the way he betrayed Jesus, he hanged himself.

But what if instead of killing himself, Judas had gone to Jesus and said, "Forgive me for what I've done!" Jesus would have forgiven him. He might even have given Judas another chance to be a disciple. Judas might have gone on to be a valuable member of the first church. He could've been a missionary or a preacher, just like the other disciples.

Jesus often used people who messed up. Just look at Peter! He denied that he even knew Jesus! But he went on to be the head of the first Christian church.

So why not Judas? If only Judas had confessed his guilt and sin to Jesus . . .

Repentance (turning away from your sin) is always better than guilt. Guilt destroys. Confessing your sins and asking for forgiveness brings new life.

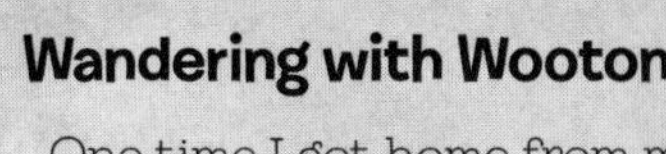

Wandering with Wooton

One time I got home from my mail route and reached into my pocket to discover an official post office paper clip! I had accidentally stolen it from work (which I'm pretty sure is a federal offense!) I ran back to the post office, but the building was closed. So I went to bed that night with the paper clip on my nightstand. I felt so guilty, I didn't get a wink of sleep! As soon as the building opened the next day, I took the paper clip back. Wow. I never like having stuff hanging over me like that! It's much better to make things right as soon as you can.

Daily Challenge

Are you feeling guilty about anything in your life right now? Are you hiding any sin that no one else knows about? Make sure you tell God about it and ask His forgiveness. And if you've hurt someone, go and make it right as soon as you can!

Devo 87

The Choice

Read Matthew 27:11–26.

Where were the five thousand people Jesus fed on the hillside? Or the ten men with leprosy who were given new life because Jesus healed them? Or the people who, just five days before, had praised Jesus as King? Were they at Jesus' trial?

The crowd in Jerusalem was given a choice. Pontius Pilate told the people he could release one of two prisoners. One was a murderer—Barabbas. The other was a man who had never hurt anyone—Jesus. He had helped, taught, healed, and loved. He was guilty of nothing except for making some of the religious leaders angry and jealous. The choice was obvious, right? And yet the crowd shouted, "Release Barabbas!"

The Bible says nothing about the few people who shouted, "Release Jesus!" But surely there would have been a few. I mean, if not, where were these people?

Where were the disciples? Jesus' best friends! Because of Jesus, they were given the great opportunity to leave their drab, broken lives. They had a powerful impact on people and brought many to faith in Jesus. Where were they?

Where was Lazarus, who would have been dead if it hadn't been for Jesus? Where were the parents of the little children Jesus loved and cared for? Wouldn't they have been on Jesus' side? What about the man born blind, whom Jesus touched and healed? Wasn't he there watching the trial with brand-new eyes?

Where would you have been? It would be nice to think that you would have been on Jesus' side. That you would have made eye contact with Him while He was standing there in front of that crowd. And maybe He would have given you a little smile when you screamed at the top of your lungs, "No! Free Jesus!"

Loquacious Learning with Eugene

According to Luke 23:49, the people who knew Jesus (presumably the twelve disciples and other friends) "stood at a distance, watching these things" when Jesus was being crucified. Only the apostle John and Jesus' mother, Mary, stood nearby. Therefore, it is reasonable to assume most people were afraid to get too close at the trial, since they could have been arrested. The question I ask myself is this: Where would I have stood?

It's impossible to know what you might have done, of course. If you had been there, you wouldn't have known what you know now—that Jesus is the Savior of the world and was about to sacrifice His life for all humankind.

The better question is "Do you know that Jesus would have done this for you, even if you hadn't been in the crowd shouting His name?" Because Jesus came for everyone, even those people who were shouting, "Crucify him!" (Matthew 27:23).

Another good question is "Are you standing up for Him today?"

Daily Challenge

How do you think Jesus felt when the crowd demanded that Pilate release Barabbas and crucify Jesus? What do you think you might have done? Gone along with the crowd? Stayed away out of fear? Had the courage to stand with Jesus?

Devo 88

Good Friday

Read Matthew 27:27–66.

Why is the day of Jesus' death called Good Friday? To answer that question, we have to look at the big picture. John 3:16 says, "God loved the world so much that he gave his one and only Son. Anyone who believes in him will not die but will have eternal life" (NIRV). From the very beginning, this was all part of God's plan. Jesus knew the day would come when He would have to sacrifice His life.

People are sinners. Romans 6:23 (NIRV) says, "When you sin, the pay you get is death." So everyone has to die to pay for their sins. But here's the great news: When Jesus died on the cross, He died in our place. He paid the penalty for our sin! But that's not all! The last part of Romans 6:23 says, "God gives you the gift of eternal life because of what Christ Jesus our Lord has done." So when we die, we'll go to heaven if we've placed our trust in Him and what He did for us on the cross.

Two huge things happened when Jesus finally died on the cross. First, Matthew 27:51 tells us, "At that moment the curtain of the temple was torn in two from top to bottom." Before this happened, the temple curtain was there to keep anybody who wasn't a special kind of priest from talking directly to God. When God miraculously tore apart the curtain, it meant that everyone could now have a personal relationship with God.

The second thing that happened is in verse 52: "Tombs broke open and the bodies of many holy people who had died were raised to life. They came out of the tombs." Dead people were raised to life. This is what will happen to us if we accept Jesus as our Savior and make Him the boss of our lives. We will die one day, but then we will join Jesus in heaven.

Connie's Corner

For a long time, I didn't want anything to do with Jesus. I thought it was all silly. But Whit taught me so much about God's love for me and how God sent His Son to die in my place. I looked at my life and how empty it was without Jesus. And suddenly it seemed silly to *not* invite Him into my heart. Whit prayed with me, and I've never been the same since.

If you haven't asked Jesus to be your Savior yet, how about today? Go to your parents, a Sunday school teacher, or a pastor, and talk about it. Then pray together and ask Jesus into your life. It will be the most important decision of your life. And it will turn this very bad Friday into a great Friday.

Daily Challenge

Each of the Gospels tells a different version of the story of Good Friday. Read one or more of the other versions: Mark 15, Luke 23, and John 19. Write a journal entry about the happiest day of your life. Now imagine you lived at the time of Jesus' death and resurrection. Write a journal entry about how that would have made you feel.

Devo 89

The Winner

Read Matthew 28:1–15.

It was probably the sunniest day ever. Don't you imagine it that way? About thirty-six hours after the ugly day on which Jesus was mocked, spit on, whipped, nailed to a cross, and stabbed, this happened. The brightest day since the sun was created. The day Jesus made the greatest comeback in world history.

Throughout His life on earth, Jesus had been in a battle for the souls of men. He battled against the religious leaders, against demons, against disease, against faithless friends. There were some dark days for Jesus up to this point. The day Satan tested Jesus in the wilderness. The day Jesus' friend John the Baptist was killed. The day the people shouted, "Crucify Him!" But today, on the brightest day in history, He won. Jesus conquered all—even death.

There was shouting, "He is alive!" The angels said it. The two Marys shouted it. The disciples probably screamed it so loud that their voices could've shattered the glassware in heaven itself. But more was alive on this day than just Jesus. This was the beginning of a new era. It wasn't just life for Him, it was life for all of us. He won, and so we all win.

There are days in life when we probably feel as if we've lost. We feel depressed. Something happens that takes the life out of us. We feel overwhelmed—by friends, by school, by the times we fail. If that ever happens, remember this day. This is the day when we win. There are days when we might feel alone with no one to turn to. But not on this day. This is the day when we know that Jesus is with us, and will never leave us. Jesus is on our team—the winning team.

Nothing can beat us if Jesus is on our team. This truth should not remain

Wandering with Wooton

I'm always in a good mood on Easter Sunday. I put on my best outfit, go to church, and hear the story about Jesus' resurrection. Then after church, I run around town shouting, "He is alive!" The only place I don't go is the Odyssey cemetery. Shouting "He is alive!" in a graveyard makes people uncomfortable–I learned my lesson there. I get a few funny looks, but I don't care. Almost everywhere I go, people know who I'm talking about, and they shout back, "Jesus is alive!" It's a great day!

hidden until Easter Sunday every year when we think about this story. This story should come to our minds every day, because we need to remind ourselves of two very important things:

He is alive! And we win.

Daily Challenge

Find a creative way to celebrate Jesus' victory over death. Draw a picture of the empty tomb. Put together a short play with your friends or siblings and perform it for your parents. Invent a game where people shout, "He is alive!"

Devo 90

The New Mission

Read Matthew 28:16–20.

Jesus spent His last moments on Earth with His disciples. There were a few more things to say before He ascended into heaven to be with His Father once again. He had a mission for them: "Go and make disciples of all nations, baptizing them in the name of the Father and of the Son and of the Holy Spirit" (Matthew 28:19).

This was Jesus' commandment to His disciples, and they took it seriously. In the book of Acts, we learn that the disciples began the first Christian church. They also spread the good news about Jesus everywhere, even to the ends of the earth.

But this mission wasn't just for the disciples. It's our mission too. Jesus wants us to spread the word about Him to as many people as we can.

What can you say to others about Jesus? Well, the book of Matthew gives you a lot of information to share.

First, you can tell people about Jesus' birth. How He came to the earth as a little baby, and people came to worship Him. Just imagine: He was their King before He could even speak a word!

You can also tell people about Jesus' teachings. Talk about the important lessons He taught in Matthew 5–7—like being salt and light, guarding against the dangers of greed, and trusting God to provide for His children.

Don't forget to mention Jesus' miracles. When He healed the sick, He proved that He has power over disease. When He calmed the storm, He proved that He has power over nature. And when He fed five thousand people with the fish and loaves, He proved that He has power over material things.

Whit's Wisdom

You've now read through the entire book of Matthew. Jesus' life on earth was fascinating, educational, miraculous, tragic, and hopeful, all at once. I hope you learned a lot and will share what you discovered with people who don't know the wonderful story of Jesus.

Tell others about how Jesus helped the disciples become leaders instead of just followers. Tell how He suffered a horrible death to save the people of the world. Tell about how He rose from the dead, conquering evil, sin, and death once and for all.

There are so many wonderful things to share about Jesus. But if this mission makes you afraid or nervous, remember something else Jesus said to His disciples: "Surely I am with you always, to the very end of the age" (Matthew 28:20).

Daily Challenge

Hopefully, by this point, you've established a routine for reading and studying your Bible every day. Don't stop! Keep reading through the next book of the Bible—Mark. And pray daily that you'll continue to learn more about Jesus!

Easter Word Search

Find the answers to the following questions. When you're finished, search for the answers in the corresponding puzzle. You'll find the words hidden frontward, backward, up, down, and diagonally.

1. In the *Odyssey* episode "Choices," Lucy felt it was wrong to write a paper on __________. (Devo 85)
2. Lucy's teacher was so impressed by her __________ that he changed her assignment. (Devo 85)
3. Romans 14:23: "Everything that does not come from faith is __________." (Devo 85)
4. __________ denied knowing Jesus, and the rooster crowed. (Devo 85)
5. Guilt destroys. Asking God for __________ brings new life. (Devo 86)
6. __________ felt so guilty for betraying Jesus that the guilt eventually caused him to kill himself. (Devo 86)
7. __________ means to turn away from your sin. (Devo 86)
8. __________ gave the crowd a choice between releasing a murderer or releasing Jesus. (Devo 87)
9. The crowd chose to release the criminal named __________. (Devo 87)
10. Jesus was crucified on which day? __________ __________. (Devo 88)
11. __________ 3:16 says, "God loved the world so much that he gave his one and only Son. Anyone who believes in him will not die but will have eternal life." (Devo 88)
12. __________ 6:23 says, "The wages of sin is death, but the gift of God is eternal life in Christ Jesus our Lord." (Devo 88)
13. The __________ in the temple was torn in two from top to bottom. (Devo 88)

14. "__________ broke open. The bodies of many holy people who had died were raised to life." (Matthew 27:52; Devo 88)
15. Jesus rose from the dead on what is now called __________ Sunday. (Devo 89)
16. When Jesus rose from the dead, many shouted, "He is __________!" (Devo 89)
17. Jesus commands His followers to "make disciples of all nations" and to __________ them "in the name of the Father and of the Son and of the Holy Spirit." (Matthew 28:19; Devo 90)
18. "And surely I am with you always, to the very __________ of the age." (Matthew 28:20; Devo 90)

E	D	D	R	E	T	E	P	S
E	N	E	J	N	E	B	I	N
R	E	T	U	V	A	N	Y	A
E	J	A	I	P	C	S	A	M
T	U	L	T	N	O	S	D	O
S	A	I	J	I	N	E	I	R
A	Z	P	O	A	V	N	R	E
E	E	S	H	T	I	E	F	P
N	V	U	N	R	C	V	D	E
E	V	O	L	U	T	I	O	N
J	B	V	R	C	I	G	O	T
U	A	E	A	A	O	R	G	A
D	R	R	B	A	N	O	B	N
A	T	O	M	B	S	F	J	C
S	A	B	B	A	R	A	B	E

Answers on page 211.

Puzzle Answer Key

Puzzle #1

Jesus' Family Tree

								D									P
						I	S	A	A	C			J	E	S	S	E
								V					E				R
			E	L	I	A	K	I	M		J	A	C	O	B		E
			L			M		D			O		O				Z
			E			M					S		N				
	A		A			I		H	E	Z	E	K	I	A	H		
	H	E	Z	R	O	N					P		A				
	A		A			A	B	I	J	A	H		H			R	
A	Z	O	R			D						U				A	
		B		J		A			J			Z	E	R	A	H	
	Z	E	R	U	B	B	A	B	E	L		Z				A	
		D		D			B		H			I		S		B	
			T	A	M	A	R		O			A	M	O	N		
				H			A		R	U	T	H		L			
							H		A					O			
						S	A	L	M	O	N			M	A	R	Y
							M							O		A	
														N		M	

Puzzle #2

The New Rules

Answers to scrambled letters: (1) James; (2) heaven; (3) synagogue; (4) Isaiah; (5) Galilee; (6) Simon; (7) Nazareth. Answer to numbered clues: Love your enemies.

Puzzle #3

Bible Code

Answers to code: A = 14; C = 18; D = 11; E = 2; G = 8; H = 15; I = 6; L = 16; N = 21; O = 4; P = 17; R = 26; S = 10; T = 20; U = 19; V = 9; W = 25; Y = 13. Answer: Do not give dogs what is sacred; do not throw your pearls to pigs.

Puzzle #4

Bible Basics Code

Answer: Everyone who hears these words of mine and puts them into practice is like a man who built his house on the rock.

Puzzle #5

Follow the Rules?

Answer: The only thing that counts is faith expressing itself through love.

Puzzle #6

Signs of the Savior

Answer: The blind receive sight, the lame walk, those who have leprosy are cured, the deaf hear, the dead are raised, and the good news is preached to the poor.

Puzzle #7

Cross-Out Code

Answer: For whoever does the will of my Father in heaven is my brother and sister and mother.

Puzzle #8
Names of Jesus

X	J	Q	**D**	Q	B	J	J	Z	X	B
Q	B	**R**	Z	J	X	Q	S	B	J	**L**
G	**O**	**D**	**A**	**N**	**D**	**M**	**A**	**N**	Q	**E**
L	Z	**C**	Z	J	B	X	**V**	Q	B	**U**
X	B	Q	**A**	X	Q	**K**	**I**	**N**	**G**	**N**
S	J	Z	B	**R**	B	J	**O**	Q	Z	**A**
H	Q	X	Z	Q	**P**	Z	**R**	X	Q	**M**
E	**T**	**E**	**A**	**C**	**H**	**E**	**R**	Z	B	**M**
P	J	Z	Q	Z	**L**	X	**N**	J	Z	**I**
H	Q	B	X	**A**	J	B	B	**T**	J	X
E	Z	J	**E**	Q	Z	Q	X	J	**E**	Q
R	X	**H**	J	B	X	B	Q	Z	B	**R**
D	**F**	**R**	**I**	**E**	**N**	**D**	J	B	X	Q

Answers: LORD; GOD AND MAN; SHEPHERD; FRIEND; HEALER; TEACHER; CARPENTER; SAVIOR; KING; IMMANUEL.

Puzzle #9
Scrambled Surprise

Answers: (1) George Mueller, (2) unimportant, (3) temper, (4) instructions, (5) temptation, (6) Joseph, (7) shepherd, (8) friendship, (9) seventy times seven, (10) grudges.

Puzzle #10

Acrostic from Matthew

Answers to question: (1) follow, (2) Mona Lisa, (3) The Vow, (4) temple, (5) last, (6) chocolate, (7) one, (8) Palm Sunday, (9) greatest, (10) salvation, (11) money (12) kingdom.

Final answer: Five thousand.

Puzzle #11

Math Code

Answer: Give to Caesar what is Caesar's and to God what is God's.

Puzzle #12

Hexagon Help

Answer: Whatever you did for one of the least of these brothers of mine, you did for me.

Puzzle #13

Easter Word Search

Answers: (1) evolution, (2) conviction, (3) sin, (4) Peter, (5) forgiveness, (6) Judas, (7) Repentance, (8) Pilate, (9) Barabbas, (10) Good Friday, (11) John, (12) Romans, (13) curtain, (14) Tombs, (15) Easter, (16) alive, (17) baptize, (18) end.

Notes

Devo 2

1. *Blue Letter Bible*, "*El Shaddai* (Lord God Almighty)," accessed November 26, 2013, http://www.blueletterbible.org/study/misc/name_god.cfm.
2. *Strong's Lexicon* s.v. "H3070, "*Yĕhovah yireh*," accessed November 26, 2013, http://www.blueletterbible.org/lang/lexicon/lexicon.cfm?strongs=H3070.
3. *Theopeida.com* s.v. "*Elohim*," accessed November 26, 2013, http://www.theopedia.com/Elohim.
4. *Strong's Lexicon* s.v. "H6005, "*Immanuw'el*," accessed November 26, 2013, http://www.blueletterbible.org/lang/lexicon/lexicon.cfm?strongs=H6005.

Devo 3

1. *International Bible Encyclopedia* s.v. "gold," accessed November 26, 2013, http://www.studylight.org/enc/isb/view.cgi?n=3846.
2. *International Bible Encyclopedia* s.v. "frankincense," accessed November 26, 2013, http://www.studylight.org/enc/isb/view.cgi?n=3549.
3. *International Bible Encyclopedia* s.v. "myrrh," accessed November 26, 2013, http://www.studylight.org/enc/isb/view.cgi?n=6163.

Devo 4

1. *World Book Online: Reference Center*, s.v. "sun," accessed November 26, 2013, http://www.worldbookonline.com.
2. *World Book Online: Reference Center*, s.v. "beetle," accessed November 26, 2013, http://www.worldbookonline.com.
3. *World Book Online: Reference Center*, s.v. "brain," accessed November 26, 2013, http://www.worldbookonline.com.

Devo 9

1. *International Bible Encyclopedia* s.v. "Fisher; Fisherman," accessed November 26, 2013, http://www.studylight.org/enc/isb/view.cgi?n=3437&search=fishermen#fishermen.

2. *The Catholic Encyclopedia* s.v. "St. Andrew," accessed November 26, 2013, http://www.studylight.org/enc/tce/view.cgi?n=718&search=Andrew#Andrew; *International Bible Encyclopedia* s.v. "Peter, Simon," accessed November 26, 2013, http://www.studylight.org/enc/isb/view.cgi?w=Peter%2C+simon; and *International Bible Encyclopedia* s.v. "John, the Apostle," accessed November 26, 2013, http://www.studylight.org/enc/isb/view.cgi?n=5047&search=John,%20the%20Apostle#John,%20the%20Apostle.

Devo 13

1. Bible History Online, "The Pharisees—Jewish Leaders in the First Century AD: Their Traditions," accessed May 21, 2013, http://www.bible-history.com/pharisees/PHARISEESTradition.htm.

Devo 17

1. Kate Bratskeir, "The Habits of Supremely Happy People," *The Huffington Post,* posted September 16, 2013, updated November 6, 2013, accessed December 24, 2013, http://www.huffingtonpost.com/2013/09/16/happiness-habits-of-exuberant-human-beings_n_3909772.html.
2. Larry Burkett, *Using Your Money Wisely: Biblical Principles Under Scrutiny* (Chicago: Moody Press, 1990), 11.

Devo 19

1. *Strong's Concordance*, s.v. "Greek: 5273, *hupokritēs*," accessed May 21, 2013, http://biblesuite.com/greek/5273.htm.

Devo 21

1. Sam McLeon, *Asch Experiments,* Simple Psychology, 2008, accessed December 24, 2013, http://www.simplypsychology.org/asch-conformity.html. See also Solomon Asch Conformity Experiments (1951): The Power of Conformity, accessed December 24, 2013, http://myclass.peelschools.org/sec/11/20135/Lessons/Sociocultural%20Studies%20Review/Conformity%20-%20Asch%20(1951).PDF

Devo 22

1. Tracy V. Wilson, "How Zombies Work," howstuffworks, accessed December 24, 2013, http://science.howstuffworks.com/science-vs-myth/strange-creatures/zombie1.htm.

Devo 23

1. Alun Palmer, "Leaning Tower of Pisa Finally Straightened and Saved from Collapse," *Mirror (UK) News*, December 14, 2010, http://www.mirror.co.uk/news/uk-news/leaning-tower-of-pisa-finally-straightened-269264.

Devo 31

1. Joshua Project, "Great Commission Statistics: Global Statistics," accessed June 10, 2013, http://www.joshuaproject.net/great-commission-statistics.php.
2. World Stadiums, "100,000+ Stadiums," accessed June 13, 2013, http://www.worldstadiums.com/stadium_menu/stadium_list/100000.shtml.

Devo 32

1. Wild Flora's Wild Gardening, "The Starfish Story," blog entry by Flora Cordis Johnson, accessed June 11, 2013, http://wildgardeners.blogspot.com/2007/04/starfish-story.html, adapted from Loren C. Eiseley, "The Star Thrower," in *The Unexpected Universe* (Orlando, FL: Harcourt Brace, 1969), 67–92.

Devo 33

1. Chel Avery, "Traditional Quaker Worship," Quaker Information Center, accessed June 13, 2013, http://quakerinfo.org/quakerism/worship.

Devo 37

1. Ace Collins, *Stories Behind the Hymns That Inspire America: Songs That Unite Our Nation* (Grand Rapids: Zondervan, 2003), 83.
2. "He's Got the Whole World in His Hands," in Collins, *Stories Behind the Hymns That Inspire America*, 85.

Devo 38

1. Simon Cannon de Bastardo, "Unusual Religious Rituals Around the World," BoontsnAll.com, September 14, 2012, http://www.bootsnall.com/articles/11-04/unusual-religious-rituals-around-the-world.html.

Devo 40

1. John Lennon and Paul McCartney, "Yellow Submarine," copyright 1966, Capitol.
2. Statistics Brain, "The Beatles Album Sales Statistics," StatisticsBrain.com, July 23, 2012, http://www.statisticbrain.com/the-beatles-total-album-sales/.

Devo 44

1. *Nelson's Complete Book of Bible Maps and Charts*, (Nashville: Thomas Nelson, 1993), 300.

Devo 45

1. Walking with Jesus Ministries, "The Parable of the Weeds," accessed June 14, 2013, http://www.wwj.org.nz/teachings/teaching.php?id=370.

Devo 46

1. Middle Ages, "Black Death," accessed June 14, 2013, http://www.middle-ages.org.uk/black-death.htm.
2. Natural History Museum, "Xenopsylla cheopis (plague flea)," accessed June 14, 2013, http://www.nhm.ac.uk/nature-online/species-of-the-day/scientific-advances/disease/xenopsylla-cheopis/index.html.
3. TheNumbers.com, "Tom Cruise," accessed June 14, 2013, http://www.the-numbers.com/person/540401-Tom-Cruise.
4. Pew Forum on Religion and Public Life, *Global Christianity: A Report and the Size and Distribution of the World's Christian Population* (Washington, DC: Pew Research Center, 2011), http://www.pewforum.org/Christian/Global-Christianity-worlds-christian-population.aspx.

Devo 48

1. K. K. Devaraj, "Our Story," Bombay Teen Challenge: Restoring Broken Lives, accessed June 17, 2013, http://bombaytc.org/our_story.html.

Devo 49

1. Bible Basics, "12 Disciples—How They Died," accessed June 17, 2013, http://biblebasics.wordpress.com/2007/02/16/12-disciples/; Billy Graham Evangelistic Association, Answers: "What happened to the original 12 disciples of Jesus?," posted July 29, 2004, http://www.billygraham.org/articlepage.asp?ArticleID=3847.
2. *Smith's Bible Dictionary*, s.v. "John the Apostle," accessed June 17, 2013, http://topicalbible.org/j/john_the_apostle.htm.

Devo 50

1. Billy Graham, *Just As I Am: The Autobiography of Billy Graham* (New York: HarperCollins, 1997), 26.

Devo 51

1. *Strong's Concordance*, s.v. "*tharseō*," accessed June 17, 2013, http://www.biblesuite.com/greek/2293.htm.

Devo 54

1. Frazer, quoted in " 'Don't End Up in Here Like Us,' Say Killers," *Edges*, no. 33: 19, www.users.globalnet.co.uk/~edges/online/issue33/p19.pdf.
2. HowStuffWorks.com, "Yeast," accessed June 18, 2013, http:// science.howstuffworks.com/life/fungi/yeast-info.htm.
3. Ibid.

Devo 56

1. Etiquette advice from Huma Khan, Rachel Kelly, and Paul Gauger, cited in and adapted from ElegantWoman.org, "Royal Etiquette: How to Greet the Queen," accessed June 19, 2013, http://www.elegantwoman.org/royal-etiquette.html.

Devo 59

1. Source for the Japanese folktale is unavailable. The author remembers the story from childhood.
2. C. Herbert Woolston, "Jesus Loves the Little Children," in Larry McCabe, *101 Three-Chord Hymns and Gospel Songs* (Pacific, MO: Mel Bay, 2008), 65.

Devo 61

1. Adapted from Margaret Feinberg, *Scouting the Divine: My Search for God in Wine, Wool, and Wild Honey* (Grand Rapids: Zondervan, 2009).
2. C. S. Lewis, *The Weight of Glory* (New York: HarperCollins, 2001), 46.

Devo 63

1. David Doege, "Brookfield Man Accused of Vandalism," *Milwaukee Journal Sentinel*, October 8, 2003, http://news.google.com/newspapers?nid=1683&dat=20031008&id=SbcaAAAAIBAJ&sjid=WEUEAAAAIBAJ&pg=5360,5707367.
2. Anne Lamott, *Traveling Mercies: Some Thoughts on Faith* (New York: Anchor Books, 1999), 134.

Devo 64

1. Pew Research Center analysis of US Census data, cited in D'Vera Cohn et al., *Barely Half of US Adults Are Married—A Record Low* (Washington, DC: Pew Social and Demographic Trends, 2011), http://www.pewsocialtrends.org/files/2011/12/Marriage-Decline.pdf.

Devo 65

1. Elisabeth Elliot, *Shadow of the Almighty: The Life and Testament of Jim Elliot* (New York: HarperCollins, 1958), 247.

Devo 67

1. Robert Novick, *Anarchy, State, and Utopia* (New York: Basic Books, 1974), 42–44.
2. Wayne Watson, "Looking Out for Number One," *How Time Flies*, copyright © 1992, Word.

Devo 68

1. Tim Gallant, "The Triumphal Entry," Biblical Studies Center, accessed July 22, 2013, http://www.biblicalstudiescenter.org/interpretation/triumphal-maccabee.htm.

Devo 72

1. "Lev Yashin," Factual World, accessed December 6, 2013, http://www.factualworld.com/article/Lev_Yashin.
2. Promethium is radioactive. See "Differences Between Lanthanides and Actinides," in "Lanthanides and Actinides," TutorVista.com, http://chemistry.tutorvista.com/inorganic-chemistry/lanthanides-and-actinides.html. See also "Promethium: The Essentials," Web Elements: The Periodic Table on the Web, accessed December 5, 2013, http://www.webelements.com/promethium/.

Devo 76

1. Christopher Hodapp and Alice von Kannon, *The Templar Code for Dummies* (Hoboken NJ: Wiley, 2007), 36.
2. Teun Koetsier and Luc Bergmans, eds., *Mathematics and the Divine: A Historical Study* (Amsterdam: Elsevier, 2005), 303.

3. Christopher Collins, *Homeland Mythology: Biblical Narratives in American Culture* (University Park, PA: Pennsylvania State University Press, 2007), 103.
4. George Browning Lockwood, *The New Harmony Communities* (Marion, IN: Chronicle, 1902), 21–22.

Devo 78

1. Leo Tolstoy, "Where Love Is, God Is," 1885, in Literature Network, http://www.online-literature.com/tolstoy/2892/.

Devo 82

1. Joni Eareckson Tada, interview by Janet Chismar, in "Joni Eareckson Tada on Prayer," Billy Graham Evangelistic Association, May 4, 2011, accessed December 5, 2013, http://billygraham.org/story/joni-eareckson-tada-on-prayer/.
2. Joni Eareckson Tada Story, "Why?," Life Story Foundation, accessed December 5, 2013, http://www.jonieareckson tadastory.com.

Devo 84

1. "October 30, 1974: Muhammad Ali Wins the Rumble in the Jungle," "This Day in History," History.com, accessed December 5, 2013, http://www.history.com/this-day-in-history/muhammad-ali-wins-the-rumble-in-the-jungle.

Devo 86

1. William Shakespeare, *Macbeth*, in "*Macbeth*: Plot Overview," SparkNotes, accessed December 9, 2013, http://www.sparknotes.com/shakespeare/macbeth/summary.html.